THE TOLPUDDLE MARTYRS

The following inscription appears on one of the posts of the Memorial Gateway, erected in 1912, outside the 'Church of the Martyrs', Tolpuddle, Dorset:

Erected in honour
of the
Faithful & Brave Men
of this Village
Who in 1834 so nobly
suffered Transportation
in the cause of
Liberty, Justice,
and Righteousness
and as a Stimulus
to our own
And future Generations.

George Loveless
James Loveless
James Hammett
Thomas Standfield
John Standfield
James Brine

THE TOLPUDDLE MARTYRS

by

MARJORIE M. FIRTH

and

ARTHUR W. HOPKINSON

With a Foreword by

RT. HON. WALTER ELLIOT M.P.

Ex-Minister of Agriculture

EP PUBLISHING LIMITED
1974

Republished 1974 by EP Publishing Limited
East Ardsley, Wakefield
Yorkshire, England

Originally published by Martin Hopkinson Ltd, 1934

ISBN 0 85409 963 8

Please address all enquiries to EP Publishing Ltd
(address as above)

Printed in Great Britain by
REDWOOD BURN LIMITED
Trowbridge & Esher

FOREWORD

IT is because the events chronicled in this book constitute a landmark in the history of agriculture in this country that I willingly accede to the request of the authors that I should contribute a short Foreword. A description of the incidents connected with the trial of the Tolpuddle labourers, its implications, and the atmosphere of the times, fittingly makes its appearance on the eve of the centenary of the trial. That trial was unquestionably an event of interest and importance to all men and women, regardless of party or creed, marking as it did a very early step in the rallying of the common people after the Industrial Revolution. But although the incident created a great impression at the time on public opinion, progress was slow and difficult. It is only on looking back that we can see how far we have come.

This is what the six Tolpuddle men would find if they were here to-day. Agricultural workers are taking an increasing part in all branches of public life. Their representatives sit with an equal number of representatives of employers on the Agricultural Wages Committees which determine the minimum wage rates in each area. They are members of the rural and county councils; they figure on the magisterial bench; they are represented on the County Agricultural Committees and on the National Councils of Agriculture. A veteran leader of agricultural workers, George Edwards, who was born within a few years of the Tolpuddle events, and who died only this month, was honoured by H.M. The King with the dignity of Knighthood, after a lifetime devoted to furthering the interests of his fellow workers; which in itself supplies the greatest evidence of the recognition by the community as a whole of the agricultural worker's full freedom to take collective action for the advancement of the welfare of himself and his fellows.

I think it must undoubtedly be said that as a result of the operations of the minimum wage machinery, the land workers' economic position to-day is considerably better than before the War, though in those times agriculture was in a more prosperous condition than it has been in the last few years. That is not to say that the worker reaps to-day a reward such as his skill and the vital nature of his activities would entitle him to, given more prosperous conditions. Agriculture was once regarded as a Cinderella among the industries of this country and the worker on the farm was generally regarded as inferior to and less skilled than, workers in other industries. Those days are gone, I hope for ever. But it is the case that all agriculturists are partners in a great industry, the greatest industry of this country, and all their fortunes are bound up with its success. The terms of a statute can lay down a wage, but it is only a prosperous agriculture that can ensure to the workers that improvement in their general position which is their just ambition.

Nearly one hundred years have passed since the six labourers of Tolpuddle were sentenced to transportation. It may perhaps be a matter for surprise that this event attracted the attention it did at a time when the public conscience was not so easily aroused as it is now, but the reason is clear; those men in their actions exhibited in a transcendent degree those qualities which have always appealed to the hearts of our people throughout its history, a passionate love of liberty, hatred of oppression, and a readiness to suffer in a just cause. That is why the story of the martyrs of Tolpuddle should be, in the words of the inscription on the gateway erected in their memory, 'a stimulus to our own and future generations'.

WALTER ELLIOT

ACKNOWLEDGMENTS

NO one can write on any matter concerning the social and industrial conditions of this country, in the last century, without being indebted to two books—*The History of Trade Unionism* by Sidney and Beatrice Webb, and *The Village Labourer* by J. L. and Barbara Hammond. Both books owe something of their completeness to the fact that they include both the man's and the woman's outlook on the problems with which they are concerned. For, as Mr. J. C. Pringle has reminded us in *The Nation's Appeal to the Housewife*, social and industrial problems can never be solved without full consideration of the woman's point of view. So in this little sketch of one incident in the history of conditions in the English countryside, we have paid the Webbs and the Hammonds the 'sincerest flattery' of imitation by collaborating in the effort to give a true and complete picture from both points of view. We gratefully acknowledge what we owe to them.

We thank, also, the Curator of the Dorset County Museum for permission to consult various documents under his care, and the manager of the

Dorset County Chronicle for the opportunity of examining the files of that old-established paper relating to the events of 1834. The Vicar of Tolpuddle has kindly placed the parish registers at our disposal, and so enabled us to verify several interesting points about the Martyrs.

Mr. W. H. Parry Okeden, a true lover of Dorset, has allowed us to make unrestricted use of his pamphlet on *The Agricultural Riots in Dorset in 1830*, and the very illuminating correspondence it contains. The same generosity has been extended by Sir Gerald Hurst, K.C., M.P., with regard to his article on *The Dorchester Labourers, 1834*, which gives an authoritative conclusion on the legal aspect of their trial. Not least are we indebted to Sir Ernest Debenham, Bart., of Briantspuddle, whose 'services to agriculture', recognized by the King, make him one of the surest guides through the mazes of agricultural policy. As an experimental and practical farmer, who has himself farmed 6,000 acres in Dorset, he can speak with experience on what to most of our statesmen is a matter of theorizing. At the same time he has the wider outlook of a man of many interests, and of one who knows that the future can only be planned on an understanding of the past. He has grudged neither time nor trouble in helping us to expand our study of what happened in 1834 into a consideration of what is happening and what may happen in the basic industry of our country. We must not forget to mention our indebtedness to Mr. Brooks' pamphlet, *Six Heroes in Chains*, and Mr. Rattenbury's romance, *The Flame of Freedom.*

In making these acknowledgments to those who have helped us, we do not lay on them any responsibility for our interpretation of the information they have so kindly supplied. At the same time we can claim that what we have written is the outcome of a study of the best available sources of information.

Finally, difficult though it is to express, we owe a very happy gratitude to Dorset. We have tried to breathe the atmosphere of this most fascinating county. We love it in all its variegated charm of downland and valley, of heaths and creeks. And we feel that by loving it, we have learned to know it and its people. The land and the labourers are inseparable. It is only by being steeped in Dorset that we can write with the understanding of sympathy about the lives of Dorset folk.

M.M.F.
A.W.H.

Michaelmas, 1933.

CONTENTS

Some village Hampden that with dauntless breast
The little tyrant of his fields withstood

CHAPTER I

1834–1934

ON March 19th, 1834, at the Dorchester Assizes, six men of unblemished character were sentenced to seven years' transportation for the technical crime of 'administering an unlawful oath'. They had made a sworn agreement, on trade union lines, to act together in trying to win a rise of wages from 7s. a week to 10s. a week. So great was the indignation aroused by the savagery of their sentence that the Government was forced to recommend that they should be granted a free pardon. But by deliberate trickery the news of their pardon was kept from them till they had served about two years of their punishment. When they returned to England they shunned the limelight; and eventually five of them settled in Canada, where they never spoke of the sufferings through which they had passed. It seemed as if they sought oblivion. To the credit of the British nation, that oblivion has been denied them; and their example of steadfast heroism has earned for them undying fame as 'The Tolpuddle Martyrs'. The hundredth anniversary of their tragedy is an opportunity for recalling something of its significance.

A centenary is nothing in itself. It matters little whether an event happened ninety-nine years ago or a hundred years ago. But the 'centenary habit' has become engrained in the lives of the present generation, and makes good news-value for the newspapers. It is not unprofitable; for it recalls the memory of men and events which might otherwise be forgotten to the notice of a hurrying and self-centred age. On the other hand there are certain dangers in the 'habit'; journalists have not always the sense of responsibility which marks the trained historian. Events may be 'written up' and coloured to catch the attention or propitiate the prejudices of readers. And when great men are commemorated by a centenary, there is an inevitable tendency to emphasize their importance by belittling their contemporaries. These dangers are particularly imminent when keeping the centenary of some event of which the consequences are still in suspense, the beginning of some religious or social movement about which men are still at variance—some saying that the event marked the first step upwards, and others that it marked the first step downwards.

Two such events are commemorated in 1933 and 1934. Everyone who reads has had the opportunity of learning about John Keble's famous Assize Sermon in July, 1833, which is reckoned as the starting-point of the Oxford Movement in the Church of England. The incident, which in 1834 marked a phase in the progress of the trade union movement in England, is less well-known. But the trial and transportation of the six Dorset labourers, known as 'The Tolpuddle Martyrs', was one of the turning-points in the social and industrial history of our country. The consequences of both these events are still with us; and those who are involved in them are apt to take a distorted view of the events themselves. Already there are murmurings of a desire to exploit the crime against the Tolpuddle labourers for party purposes, just as there was a danger of a similar sort that party societies in the Church of England might try to use the 1933 centenary for the furtherance of their own ends.

The leaders of the Tolpuddle Movement were as

different from the leaders of the Oxford Movement as Tolpuddle is different from Oxford. But they, also, were great men fighting in a great cause. They, too, were above the petty schisms of party and self-seeking. It is by giving them their due, as heroes not of a class but of a nation, that those who celebrate their memory may share a common pride and unite in a national tribute of praise and gratitude. There is no reason, we believe, why the happy result of the centenary celebration of the Oxford Movement, in banishing misunderstandings between men having the same aims at heart, should not find its counterpart in the very different celebration which in 1934 is to renew interest in an event of 1834 so notable that it shocked the public conscience into an activity which has made the repetition of such an event unthinkable. The crime which the governing classes committed against the six labourers of Tolpuddle would not find a single defender among the governing classes of to-day. The persecuted have converted the persecutors. Martyrdom, as always, has proved worth while. But here again, as in the 1933 centenary, there must be a readiness to learn from history. We must get back to fundamentals, and find in them the underlying truths for which men of good-will can always strive, though they may seek the same ends by very various means. It would be a thousand pities if the centenary of the Tolpuddle Martyrs were exploited on behalf of some religious or political sectarianism. The celebration should draw men together, not drive them apart. The truest honour we can render to the dauntless six is to celebrate their memory not merely as martyrs for trade unionism or for Nonconformity, but as martyrs for Freedom. It is doubtful indeed whether they would recognize in the trade unionism of to-day the simple right of combination, or in the Nonconformity of to-day the claim to liberty of conscience, for which they suffered. In this suggestion there is no attempt to stir up debate, nor to cloud over the outstanding facts that five of the six derived their inspiration from the old-fashioned Methodism in which they had been nurtured, and that one outcome of their stand for freedom has been the progress of the trade union movement. Methodists and trade unionists have special cause for celebrating this centenary, special but not exclusive: the whole nation may be drawn closer together in the cause of freedom by a united recognition of the fight, the martyrdom, and the victory of the six men of Tolpuddle.

Oxford and Tolpuddle are poles apart. The

centenaries of 1933 and of 1934 have little in common. On the surface, one was a spiritual and intellectual awakening in the religious life of a university town among men of learning and refinement, with far-reaching consequences which do not concern this comparison. The other was the resistance of six labourers in a remote village to the petty tyranny of some local Jacks-in-office—also with far-reaching consequences. Nevertheless, though the events were so dissimilar, it is not altogether fanciful to trace some likeness in their causes and results. The Tolpuddle martyrs and the Tractarian fathers alike were up against the *vis inertiæ* of Whiggism in State and Church. The Whig policy of letting sleeping dogs lie was carried to such extremes that any dog who showed signs of awakening was knocked on the head. The dogs were not even allowed to eat of the crumbs which fell from the rich man's table. The rulers of Church and State, whatever might be their particular party label, were sunk in a sordid conservatism. Stagnation and privilege were the pivots of their existence. They were not deliberately wicked; but when they became frightened they became cruel, with all the relentless cruelty of unimaginative natures. Whether it was the refinement of cruelty in their treatment of Pusey or the crude brutality of their treatment of Loveless, the motive was the same—they were hag-ridden with Fear.

The love of stagnation was not the monopoly of any one class. It is a coincidence not without interest that the neighbourhood of Tolpuddle provides an illustration of how a Churchman, who was not content to share the stagnation with which he was surrounded, suffered for venturing to be awake. Piddlehinton is only a few miles from Tolpuddle, another typical Dorset village. In 1838 a young priest, who had been influenced by the Oxford Movement, was appointed rector: he afterwards became famous as 'Canon Carter of Clewer'. He had been inspired with high ideals of the pastoral life by reading the *Tracts for the Times*. 'In reading them,' he says, 'I felt a sense of interest and earnestness in religious doctrines I had not known before.' He was a young man eager to serve God and his flock. But when the neighbouring clergy heard that the new rector neither shot, nor fished, nor hunted, one of them exclaimed aghast: 'What then will he find to do?' He found plenty to do, but his efforts at reform were wrecked on the rock of conservatism. It was bad enough when he substituted a harmonium for the instrumentalists who led the church music. But when he proposed to substitute a Clothing Club for the ancient, rectorial gift of a mince-pie, a loaf of bread, and a quart of old ale to every man, woman, child, and baby in arms of the parish, the storm broke. Labourers and farmers alike were opposed to these new-fangled notions. And after a rather disastrous ministry of four years, the future saint was driven from Dorset.

The men who nearly broke the heart of their rector at Piddlehinton were not deliberately wicked men. They were dull men. The men who brought about the transportation of the Tolpuddle labourers were not deliberately wicked men. They were dull men. The heroes of these centenaries of 1833 and 1834 are not made any whiter by painting their adversaries blacker than they really were. Moreover, if you make people of the past incredibly black, you foster the illusion that no such people exist now; and so you lose one of the pricelessly valuable warnings of history. No one can doubt that there are dull people in 1934, even among magistrates and church wardens; a true reading of history proves how dangerous they are.

It is easy for professional historians to treat the keeping of centenaries with a high-browed scorn. But History is a science of practical value, and any means of bringing home its lessons to the ordinary citizen are for the good of the commonwealth. The lessons must be fairly interpreted, and this requires care, for there is always a tendency, when popularizing history in this way, to present the incident commemorated with the lurid highlights of melodrama. The black is made blacker than any black we know; the white is made whiter than any white we know. The crudeness of the colouring deceives us into imagining that the subfusc world in which we live is a different world, and that the people whom we commemorate at centenaries were unreal people, and certainly not men of like passions with ourselves. So history only too often becomes prostituted to propaganda. It is with this danger in view that we have set out to write an unbiassed account of an event which proved to be a turning-point in the history of the English people—and to praise famous men, not because they were superhuman or foresaw how what they did in 1834 would affect the life of 1934, but because at a certain time and in a certain place and with all the limitations of their ordinary humanity, they saw the right and were ready to bear their witness in the cause of Freedom. It is doing them an injustice to claim them as demagogues, the protagonists of some political or religious policy, the instigators of modern class-warfare. They were just simple Christians doing the duty which lay nearest to hand.

That low man seeks a little thing to do,
  Sees it and does it:
This high man, with a great thing to pursue,
  Dies ere he knows it.
That low man goes on adding one to one,
  His hundred 's soon hit:
This high man, aiming at a million,
  Misses an unit.

But whatever Browning may imply as to the value of the high man's unfulfilled aspirations, it is the low man doing the little things who ensures the progress of the workaday world. As St. Gregory said, 'A little thing is a little thing; but a little thing well done is a very big thing.' The low men of Tolpuddle did their little thing well. Their witness resulted in a very big thing. But we must not attribute to them an understanding and a foresight which were not theirs. Their own statement of their case suggests nothing of the demagogue. It reminds us, rather, of the forthright simplicity of such a master of virile English as Abraham Lincoln. We must be content, and more than content, to accept the statement of their spokesman: 'We have injured no man's reputation, character, person, or property; we were uniting together to preserve ourselves, our wives and our children from utter degradation and starvation.'

This statement requires no embroidery; it is clear, definite, and complete. For the whole affair was a simple drama played on an obscure stage. No kings or nobles were involved: there was no pageantry of battle. Nor is there any excuse for pretending that the event was important except for the issues involved. We shall not keep the centenary better by dressing it up in trappings of imaginative rhetoric. It is undoubtedly tempting, for instance, to compare the Assize of 1834 with the Bloody Assize of 1685, Judge Williams with Judge Jeffreys, the victims of one with the victims of the other. It is true that the prisoners in each case have a claim to our admiration for their courage. The Dorset peasants were described as 'the bravest of Monmouth's rude army'. And it is true that the Dorchester Assize became proverbial for savagery; the percentage of prisoners punished was far higher than at either Taunton or Exeter.

But though at the later trial the prisoners were equally brave men, and the sentence cruel, the legal aspect of the matter was quite different, and the manner of the Court far more decent. There is, of course, a superficial similarity; the court at Dorchester, which Judge Jeffreys had caused to be draped with blood-red hangings, was the same; the judge's sentence was harsh; the prisoners were the victims of terror and injustice. But the comparison between the two Assizes, though specious and attractive, is utterly misleading. It is unfair to the judge, and it is unfair to the prisoners. The scattered runagates of Monmouth's Rebellion were partisans of a cause in which the risks of failure were known. Misguided they might be, but they knew enough to understand that rebels take their lives in their hands. It was right that they should be punished. It would have been wise as well as merciful if they had been let off lightly; for they were Englishmen and all further danger of rebellion was extinct. It was the brutality of the judge, who gloatingly sentenced to death two hundred and ninety-two of the three hundred prisoners brought before him, rather than any worthiness of his victims, which has filled each succeeding generation with horror. Whereas in the drama of the 1834 Assize, it is not any villainous judge who occupies the centre of the stage, but six heroic prisoners. It is they who win our sympathy, stalwart God-fearing men, yet condemned to a life-long punishment (for few ever returned from seven years transportation) for an offence which, by a legal subterfuge, was invented by their enemies. The rebels of 1685 got more than they deserved. The reformers of 1834 did not deserve punishment at all. But the judge's hand was forced, and he acted with a severity which seems to have been alien to his character.

Judge Jeffreys was a butcher in ermine, a bully who delighted in cruelty. Baron Williams was nothing of the sort: and it is unfair and untrue to say of him, as one writer has said, 'the only thing for which he stands in history is this one act of savagery, and he ranks in the records with Judge Jeffreys alone as an unjust judge. . . . He remains for ever as the outstanding and shining example of the party-hack turned loose on the Judges' bench. Not often in our island story has such infamy been perpetrated.' The truth is that he was 'painstaking and conscientious'[1] as a judge, a highly-cultivated man, and no time-server; for he had alienated the support of Lord Eldon and jeopardized his own chances of advancement by his outspoken criticism of methods of administration

[1] Dictionary of National Biography

in the Court of Chancery. Neither is there any proof of the accusation that he was specially chosen and promoted by the Home Secretary, Lord Melbourne, to perpetrate a dastardly act of injustice. He was a prejudiced man, as all men of his time and class were prejudiced; but there was justification for his allowing the prisoners to be tried under the Mutiny or Unlawful Oaths Act of George III (37 Geo. III 123), though it was passed specifically to deal with the Mutiny of the Nore, 1797. The legal aspect of the matter is convincingly set forth by Sir Gerald Hurst, K.C., in a fair-minded article in *The English Historical Review* for January, 1925, in which he criticizes the sentence rather than the verdict on the prisoners: 'Their conviction appears to have been warranted by the language of the Unlawful Oaths Act, for it is still treated as a good authority in modern textbooks on criminal law. That the law should have been invoked so ardently and enforced to the extreme limit of its penalties by a judge with Whig sympathies and justified by a Cabinet which included Grey, Melbourne, Russell and Brougham, needs more comment.' In fairness to Williams as an interpreter of the law, it is well just to give some explanation of his decision as to the applicability to the Tolpuddle case of a statute which was undoubtedly passed to deal with a situation no longer existing. Its preamble recites that the need for it had arisen through the attempts of evil and ill-disposed persons to incite His Majesty's forces and others to mutiny and sedition. The legal decision given by Judge Williams in this case, *Rex v. Loveless and others*, was that the preamble does not limit the orbit of the statute to oaths administered for the purposes of mutiny and sedition; that any association the members of which are bound by oath not to disclose its secrets is an unlawful combination for whatever purpose or object it may have been formed; and that therefore the administration of an oath not to reveal anything done in such an illegal society offends against the statute. This interpretation has been and is accepted by many fair-minded lawyers: it reflects no discredit on Williams as a judge. The matter of its application in certain cases and not in others—to the Friendly Society of Agricultural Labourers and not to the Freemasons—is another question.

The trial was, in fact, just an incident of a long political campaign. Williams was an instrument of the Whig policy of repression. Melbourne, apparently the *fons et origo mali*, was himself the willing victim of circumstances; he believed, as all his friends believed, that nothing but the continuance of the Whig domination could save the country from going to the dogs. When a class has acquired the habit of tyranny, when three generations have been brought up in an atmosphere of complete self-righteousness, it is difficult for individuals to break away from the traditions of their class. There may be no excuse for the tradition; but there is some excuse for the individual. Without any desire to whitewash Williams or Melbourne, it may nevertheless be permissible to question whether they were as black as they were painted by their victims. And it is doubtful, as we shall see later, whether Loveless's diary is as trustworthy an account of his trial as the official records.

The real villains of the piece were Frampton and his fellow squires. They instigated the prosecution, they marked down the victims, they worked on the fears of the Government and its agents. Frampton, who lived within a few miles of Tolpuddle, must have known that the employers of the doomed labourers were satisfied with their work and their conduct. After the riotings of previous years the rumour of secret societies and unlawful oaths might rouse a not unjustifiable panic in the countryside. But in this particular case, it was not just a vague and terrifying rumour; the squires knew the men whom they were out to condemn. They may have been nervous about what might happen in Dorset, but they cannot have been carried away by panic at what was happening in Tolpuddle. Two Methodist lay-preachers and their four friends, sober, hard-working men, were not likely to hold the Framptons of the neighbourhood in terror of their lives, nor to cause much mortality in the ranks of the yeomanry who were always at hand to quell disturbances when required by the magistrates. No! The squires were men who sinned against knowledge; and even if they were partially the victims of a rotten system they could not shelter entirely behind the plea of ignorance. They were doing the cruellest possible injury to men whom they did not like, not because they knew them to be a danger, but because they did not like them and their opinions.

But what about the much-abused clergy? Most of them were prejudiced against 'enthusiasm' in religious matters. They took their tone from their Whig masters. And they were made uncomfortable, and so resentful, by 'ranters' like George Loveless, whose success exposed the futility of the idle shepherds. But there is no evidence that

Thomas Warren, the vicar of Tolpuddle in 1834, was a participant in the crime against the martyrs. The evidence either way is scanty, but at first he seems to have stood up for the labourers of his parish in their claims for a rate of wages equal to that obtaining in the neighbouring counties. However, his support was short and ineffective. A possible explanation for his speedy change of front suggests itself—that he had humanity enough to approach the farmers on behalf of their workmen, but he had not courage enough to face the squires when they joined issue and protested that an attempt to get a living wage meant a sinister conspiracy against State and Church.

It has been necessary to give this preliminary warning against prejudice and propaganda, to plead for some consideration of various points of view, because the events at Tolpuddle cannot fail to arouse horror and resentment which may distort judgment. Furthermore, the righteous indignation aroused must be directed into right channels. It is no use exculpating the selfishness or failure of one political party in 1934 by denouncing the sins of some other political party in 1834. Just because possession is nine points of the law men are always tempted to strain the tenth point in their own favour. Therefore the men of to-day like to imagine that they are immune from the brutalities that disgraced their ancestors, and to make scapegoats of certain individuals of the past age, instead of acknowledging that human nature is much the same, as regards its temptations, from age to age. We may have subtler methods than the Whig leaders and their tools, but we are not more free than they were from repeating the advice that 'it is expedient for us, that one man should die for the people, and that the whole nation perish not'. Nor is this attitude confined to one class or party. Freedom, for which the Tolpuddle Martyrs suffered, is not the monopoly of democracy. It lives in every man's respect for every man, whatever form of government obtains. It is because the greatness of this truth is magnificently emphasised in the events of 1834 that we have tried in the following pages to set forth a true record of the events, how they arose, what they implied, and what are the fruits to be reaped.

CHAPTER II

THE ATMOSPHERE OF THE EPISODE

IN two later chapters we shall try to give a clear and unbiassed account of the events which are commemorated in the Centenary of 1934. In this chapter and in Chapter V, we shall try to trace back from the events to their causes, and give some indication of the background against which they took place.

Freedom was in the air: not only was the Church trying to shake itself free from a degrading Erastianism, but also, in the same year that the Oxford Movement began, the anti-slavery campaign of Wilberforce and his friends achieved its outstanding success. In August, 1833, slavery was declared to be illegal throughout the British possessions. This was the greatest and most significant event of the time, and marked a new epoch in national thought and life. It must undoubtedly have had its repercussions even in the remote villages of

Dorset. Labourers trying to live on 7s. a week, subject to every kind of petty tyranny at the hands of the local magnates, could scarcely help wondering why some of the sympathy shown for the negroes of the West Indies could not be extended to the white slaves of England. A slave in the plantations was at least an article of value; it was not a sound economic policy to let him starve to death. But no one had any care for the agricultural labourer. Perhaps, indeed, less was known about his hardships than what Wilberforce had caused to be known about the hardships of the 'middle-passage' or the sugar-fields. It would be unfair to attribute to heartlessness what was in fact the result of ignorance. For the isolation of country life in England a hundred years ago is difficult for us to realize. Transport and communications were in an elementary state. It is true that there were a few good turnpike roads, and that one of the marvels of the age was the existence of stage-coaches which were able to maintain an average speed (weather and other circumstances permitting) of twelve miles an hour. Sailors and soldiers returning to their native villages could tell of a wider world, into which their voyages and campaigns had taken them. And probably John Wesley's amazing activity in journeying throughout the country, and his encouragement of itinerant lay-preachers, who went from village to village in their own neighbourhood, had begun to do a good deal towards generating a more extended community spirit. There is little doubt, too, that Cobbett's *Political Register*, a racey newssheet issued in the cause of freedom and good farming, was widely read, and welded together the victims of Whig misrule. But it is easy to understand that these influences counted for little if they are compared with railways, daily newspapers, cheap letter-post, telegraphs, and wireless. Any picture of life in the early nineteenth century must be painted against a background of isolation which is nowadays almost incomprehensible.

The novels of the time give an insight into this state of affairs. Jane Austen, though writing mainly about the educated classes who were able to travel to Bath or London, makes it clear that the normal life outside the big towns was an isolated life. In *Persuasion*, she relates how Anne Eliot went to stay with her relations, the Musgroves, and how utterly it cut her off from her own family and her previous surroundings: 'The Mr. Musgroves had their own game to guard and to destroy: their own horses, dogs and newspapers to engage them: the females were fully occupied in all the other common subjects of housekeeping, neighbours, dress, dancing, and music. She acknowledged it to be very fitting that every little social commonwealth should dictate its own methods of discourse; and hoped, ere long, to become a not unworthy member of the one she was transplanted into. With the prospect of spending at least two months at Uppercross, it was highly incumbent on her to clothe her imagination, her memory, and all her ideas in as much of Uppercross as possible.' *And Uppercross was only three miles from her own home, Kellynch.*

It is well to realize this isolation of village life if we are to understand something of the atmosphere in which the Tolpuddle tragedy took place. When the chief source of news is rumour, there can be little value in the reports which penetrate from village to village, or from some lonely farmstead to the squire's back door. Nor did such reports lack exaggeration. It is not surprising, therefore, that rural England was panicky in the early years of the nineteenth century. In Dorset especially there had been rumours of invasion by the dreaded 'Boney': and when that danger was dissipated after Waterloo, there were rick-burnings, machine breakings, and the terrifying exploits of 'Captain Swing', the mysterious instigator of these troubles. Mysterious he might be, but he was very real to the imagination of dwellers in scattered farms and cottages. His letters of warning played havoc with the nerves of country-folk: for they were usually followed by some damage to property or person. And though no one knew who wrote the letters, or whether the exploits attributed to him were the work of one man or of many, his name was enough to shatter all confidence in security. So fear added an artificial isolation to a natural isolation. Men were not outspoken with one another (might not one be talking to 'Captain Swing'?): they grew more and more mistrustful and suspicious. What should have been movements of fellowship were driven underground and became secret societies. All the natural secretiveness of the yokel was transmuted by fear into the poison of suspicion. The labourers of Tolpuddle were betrayed by the labourers of the next village, Affpuddle; they were deserted by their employers, the farmers; and they were persecuted by the neighbouring landed gentry, who should have been their natural protectors. Dorset should have stood by Dorset.

It is difficult to say how far George Loveless and his companions were influenced by this atmosphere of suspicion. Only a spurious kind of hero-worship would claim that they were entirely immune from the frailties of their time. It must be owned, however, that their doings and their characters have been grievously obscured by the partisanship of the writers who have professed to record their story. The four elder men seem to have been a grim lot. Starvation in this world, and hell-fire in the next, were big realities which occupied their minds to the exclusion of gentler qualities of humour and refinement. But men are not betrayed into the meanness of suspicion or of panic by big realities. Whatever else these labourers may have lacked, they did not lack courage. It was of necessity that the Friendly Society of Agricultural Labourers should be a secret society, but there was nothing furtive or clandestine about its founders. And if secrecy and esoteric ritual be crimes, the Freemasons and Oddfellows had and have a heavy burden of guilt upon them. In fact, there is little doubt that the early trade unions borrowed a good deal of their ritual and their method of secret initiation from the Oddfellows. The Webbs, in their *History of Trade Unionism*, describe how admission to the Builders' Union involved a lengthy ceremony conducted by the officers of the lodge—the 'outside and inside tylers', the 'warden', the 'president', 'secretary', and 'principal conductor'—and taken part in by the candidates and members of the lodge. They tell of an opening prayer, and religious hymns sung at intervals, and how the actual initiation consisted of questions and responses in quaint doggerel between the officers and the candidates. Officers clothed in surplices, inner chambers into which the candidates were admitted blindfolded, a skeleton, drawn sword, battle-axes and other mystic 'properties' enhanced the sensational solemnity of this fantastic performance. It is noteworthy that the secret rites which formed a damning part of the accusation against the Tolpuddle men were, in a crude form, just the rites which were part of the stock-in-trade of the trade unions of the time. They were not indigenous in country places, though they must have made a special appeal to the rural mind, but they were imported from headquarters. For instance, two delegates from the Grand National Consolidated Trades Union were arrested by the police at Exeter and found to be furnished with 'two wooden axes, two large cutlasses, two masks, and two white garments or robes, a large figure of Death with the dart and hour-glass, a Bible and Testament'. The two delegates who visited Tolpuddle in the autumn of 1833 to coach Loveless in his part as a trade union leader were presumably furnished with similar 'properties' and taught him their use.

All this romantic secrecy was transplanted to congenial soil, for at that time there were few counties in England where more went on beneath the surface of everyday life than in Dorset. There was much traffic along the lanes by night. Villagers who heard the tramp of pack-horses or the rumble of wheels knew that the smugglers of Poole Harbour were abroad, but they were well advised to stay in bed and take no notice. The 'free-traders' were loyal to one another and exacted a dire vengeance on anyone who prated about their doings. They not only kept the villagers in a kind of terrorism, but they persuaded the farmers and squires to wink at their activities. The fashionable Whig policy of letting sleeping dogs lie could not find more prudent expression than in the choice between peace with the chance of finding a keg of good brandy or a packet of tobacco or silk outside the back door in the early morning, and a policy of interference which might lead to broken fences, strayed cattle, or burned ricks, if not to personal injury. The magistrates were for the most part willing to condone what they could not control, a secret network of contraband trade whereby some of them made profit. As a general rule the country-folk and the smugglers were content to live and let live; they respected one another's secrets. But in the north of the county there was a lawless community of quite a different sort. Cranborne Chase was the last tract in England to lie entirely outside the confines of law and order. It is a Chase of primitive woodland, of yews and of warrens, not greatly changed from what it was in the days when the Plantagenet kings hunted in it. As late as 1830 it was reckoned that from 12,000 to 20,000 deer harboured there. How many criminals and vagabonds it sheltered is unknown ; but it was the plague-spot of the countryside. Feuds and vendettas were only too frequent; and the law of the land was defied with impunity by small and great. The King's writ did not run. It had become a sort of Alsatia: families were brought up therein trained to theft and pillage, and accustomed to every kind of vice from birth.

Dorset, then, was far from being a county as it is so often depicted—somnolent, pastoral, and peaceful—the home of:

> Men whose lives glided on, like rivers that
>   water the woodlands
> Darkened by shadows of earth, but reflecting
>   an image of heaven.

On the contrary, it was like a quicksand, smooth and calm enough on the surface, but with hidden dangers underneath. The events of February, 1834, were the inevitable outcome of a state of affairs which must be thoroughly apprised if those events and their significance are to be understood. We have tried to give an impression of the isolation, the mistrust, and the strange romantic underground happenings which marked the life of a village like Tolpuddle in those days. It remains to say something about the ideals which animated the heroes of the time and place.

Freedom was their watchword. It was no temporary outburst of resentment that caused George Loveless to write, on the day of his condemnation:

> We raise the watchword 'Liberty';
> We will, we will, we will be free.

It was the proclamation of the creed for which he and his fellows were ready to live or die. They were in revolt against the social, religious and economic tyranny which kept them slaves in fact if not in name. But they were men who fought for something rather than against something, constructive not destructive revolutionaries. In religion, though bitter and rather unfair in their wholesale condemnation of the Church, they stood for something positive, the freedom of each individual in direct approach to God. So, too, in their claim to the right of collective bargaining to secure a fair day's wage for a fair day's work, they were inspired by the thought of economic freedom for themselves and their families. And if they were not prepared to play the part of sycophant to the squire and the parson it was because they felt it to be a degradation of their ideal of freedom. There could be no greater mistake, however, than to imagine that any one class had a monopoly of the watchword 'Freedom'. In the nineteenth century, the fight for freedom was one in which most well-meaning Englishmen had some share. But it was a campaign which took strange shapes. The employers of labour claimed freedom to deal individually with their workmen; they resented the 'tyranny' of trade unions. They claimed freedom from interference with their methods of conducting an industry—hence the scandal of child-labour, 'sweating', and long hours. Freedom in trade was becoming a popular political catchword; and the *laissez faire* ('hands off competition') school of economists was paramount in Manchester and the North. Many crimes have been committed in the name of Liberty. The great and golden image of Freedom may have had feet of clay. But all men, sincerely or in pretence, worshipped it.

This is almost incredible to the post-War generation. Freedom is no longer the rallying cry of noble souls. And even those institutions which owe their origin to the craving for freedom are in danger of denying their own principles. Could any more striking instance of this danger be given than that of an incident which happened at the 1933 annual conference of the Methodists—the denomination to which five of these six apostles of freedom belonged? It was proposed at that conference in all seriousness that, 'if any candidate [for the ministry] has entered into a matrimonial engagement, the superintendent [of the circuit] shall furnish a written statement as to the suitability of his fiancée'. It is difficult to imagine a more complete violation of all right of individual freedom than to make a man's choice of his wife subject to the approval of some superintendent, whose qualifications for the responsibility are not guaranteed. The proposal was thrown out; but it is significant that it should ever have been brought in. This is, of course, an extreme instance; but nothing is more certain that that nowadays most men fear the responsibility of independence, and leave it to the few to exploit that fear. Lenin, Hitler, or Mussolini are not liberators, leaders of a nation or class in the fight for freedom, as were so many of the heroic figures of old; they are what the modern world loves to call 'super-men'. The very bestowal of such a title shows how ready the post-War generation is to accept the yoke of slavery. It is not, of course, slavery for slavery's sake, but slavery for efficiency.

Not only in industry, but in every walk of life it is the cry for efficiency which has ousted the cry for freedom. *Propter vitam vivendi perdere causas* has no terrors for the modern mind. The only question asked about any policy is: 'Will it work?' This pragmatism has worked. It has achieved its appropriate reward; it has produced two heads of corn where one grew before. It has choked the world with goods. But it has not achieved the task of bestowing those goods on the men and women who need them, nor of training those who have them to use them aright. The world will never be saved by efficiency alone. The present world-chaos is partly the result of our forgetting that freedom is the birthright of humanity. Hence the importance of Tolpuddle; for it is impossible to understand why the transportation of six Dorset labourers roused so universal a protest throughout England, a hundred years ago, unless we remind ourselves that at the time, freedom meant all that efficiency means to us, and perhaps a good deal more. Thousands of working-men felt that the six were indeed martyrs in the cause which seemed to them the most sacred of all.

On the other hand, the minority in power, though they paid lip-service to freedom, were resolved to make it their own monopoly. They expected the poets of the day to write Odes to Liberty; they read what the philosophers or economists of the day had to say about it; but they were terrified at the type of freedom which the French Revolution had let loose. It was that which lay at the back of all their fears. Every stirring of democracy was to them a sort of nightmare of tumbrils and the guillotine. The tense atmosphere of hope and fear, centring round the conception of freedom, was general throughout the country. It requires a wise use of the imagination to discover what would be the reaction to it of a Dorset village. Tolpuddle, for instance, is deep-rooted in the past. It finds its focus at the ancient parish church, in which there is a carved effigy of Philip the Priest, dating from about 1100. But the place is still older; for it derives its name from Thola, wife of King Canute's Master of the Household. And from the days of Thola till towards the close of the eighteenth century the chief event to disturb the even tenor of country life had been the Black

Death, which did not in fact affect the western counties so seriously as the eastern. Other circumstances conspired to make Tolpuddle unchanging. There seems to have been no big estate nor resident squire in the parish; which means that the farmers, handicraftsmen and labourers would form a little commonwealth, with their own traditions and convictions—self-contained, normal and essentially English. At the same time, while history and tradition made for changelessness, geography saved the village life from dull uniformity. Tolpuddle, like so many of the parishes of Dorset, has a pleasing variety of landscape: it is not all a sleepy hollow, but borders on the open downland towards Milborne on the north and the wild heaths of Egdon towards Bere Regis on the east. Such a variety of landscape, and indeed of climate, does something to mitigate the stolidity which townsfolk attribute to the yokel. Nor must the religious factor be left out in trying to picture the outlook of the villagers, and realize the atmosphere which they breathed. They lived round the church; it enshrined that sense of continuity which is so comforting to the rustic mind. They were brought to the church to be christened or buried; they came to the church to be married. The church was a power in their subconsciousness; but it was static. Whereas Wesleyanism was dynamic; it introduced an interest and a force into village life which must be taken into account. It would be a mistake to think of the villagers as living in a state of mental stagnation. It is nearer the truth to say that many circumstances combined to make them alert.

No doubt affairs of Church and State were discussed at the inn, or at the mill, or in the village street; for Tolpuddle does not consist of isolated homesteads but of a sociable string of dwellings in which there could be no escape from neighbourliness and gossip. One may imagine that in such a community the horrors of the French Revolution would cause a reaction of disgust and fear. But the ideals of Liberty, Equality, and Fraternity, which lay behind the Revolution would fall on congenial soil among the sturdy Dorset villagers. At the same time, circumstances were so different in Tolpuddle, where there was no tyrannical overlord, from the state of affairs which roused the peasants of France to revolt, that the ultimate influence of the French Revolution must have been just to stir up vague aspirations after Freedom. There would not be, in the village life, the same feeling of insecurity and reaction of fear as that which made the squirearchy so bitter. The next world-event to make impact on Tolpuddle could be summed up in one word, 'Buonaparte'. No county which bordered on the English Channel was exempt from terror of the bugbear of Europe. Weymouth, Bridport, Lyme Regis were all possible points of invasion. And 'Boney' had attributed to him diabolical cunning and a superhuman power of conveying huge armies across treacherous seas with incredible speed. Here was a fear which drew all Englishmen closer together. But the uniting force of a common political feeling was negatived by an economic disruption. The Napoleonic wars did more than rouse patriotism; they raised prices. The landowners and the farmers were in league to exploit the War, and depress the condition of the labourers, to their own advantage. They upset traditional methods of cultivation in favour of anything that would bring them higher profits. And as they tried to debar the workers from any share in their good fortune, resentment arose, not only against the selfish employers but against the instruments of their new-fangled methods. Furthermore the employers were discovering that machinery made them much less dependent on their workmen: they required fewer, so they could choose the more docile. The unemployed problem began to loom larger in agriculture. The grim spectre of starvation haunted men in the midst of an unprecedented prosperity of the very industry which should have employed them, a prosperity which they felt they had the right to share. They foolishly put themselves in the wrong by venting their rage on the machines instead of tackling the tyranny which was entrenched behind them. The sense of change was in the air, a new epoch was opening up; and small events assumed a significance and an importance which would scarcely have been theirs had they occurred in less critical times. In such an atmosphere the Tolpuddle tragedy exploded like a bomb.

CHAPTER III

WHAT HAPPENED AT TOLPUDDLE

TOLPUDDLE is one of a group of Dorset villages that lie scattered along the winding length of the River Puddle, whose name each shares in one form or another. Puddletrenthide may carry off the palm for beauty; Puddletown may claim the most important strategic position and buildings most worthy of architectural consideration; but Tolpuddle alone has a place in the annals of national history. There is nothing particularly romantic or conspicuous about the village itself. It lies on the present highway between Poole and the West Country, and consists of a long village street with a straggle of cottages at intervals on either side; and the beautiful church on the rising ground commands a satisfying view of the water-meadows dozing along the margin of the Puddle stream. The whole district is the very quintessence of rusticity. Even now, the traffic which passes along the main road seems scarcely to affect the stolid life of these remote hamlets, but a hundred years ago they must have been entirely isolated from the growing town-life of England. It is strange, then, that six Tolpuddle working-men should have been marked out for the distinction of suffering for a 'Cause'.

Little is known of the early life of any of these men whose story we are attempting to recount, except that they were all natives of Tolpuddle. The name of Standfield appears in the Church Registers in 1720, nearly as far back, in fact, as the records are carried. Lovelesses and Brines enter the lists not many years later, whilst the Hammetts seem to be the most recent comers, the first family baptism taking place in the church in 1777. (One is tempted to digress and discourse on the airy and irresponsible manner and method of keeping registers in those days, and even the Tolpuddle books reveal inaccuracies here and there. For instance the Lovelesses spelt their own name thus in 1786, but successive vicars evidently preferred the older orthography—Lovelace—till twenty years or more later. The mother of George Loveless appears as Dinah or Diana, alternatively, under the fairly frequent entries of her name, as her children were christened. But what's in the spelling of a name? Even the Dean and Chapter of Christ Church, Oxford, must have argued thus, since in writing an order anent burials in 1778, they lightheartedly designate the village as Tollpudell.) The men were all connected by marriage in one way or another; James Hammett was brother-in-law to the Lovelesses, and James Brine later became son-in-law to old Thomas Standfield. All were farm-labourers and were well-known as being honest, hard-working, and reliable servants. Moreover, they must have been above the general level in intelligence and education for those days. George Loveless, his brother James, and Thomas Standfield, were all Methodist preachers of repute in Tolpuddle and the surrounding villages. Less is known of the other three—James Hammett, John, son of Thomas Standfield, and James Brine, but none was wholly illiterate.

George Loveless was their natural leader. His faith in his religion was deep and sincere and he was blessed with a power of personality with which to impress his words on his hearers. His must have been an unusual character—independent, courageous and far-seeing; he was not one to remain inert when there was work to be done, and he was the prime mover in the local agitation for an increase in the general rate of wage to be paid throughout the county. If we would grasp the significance of his action in any degree, we must realize some of the recent changes that had taken place in the lives of the agricultural labourers, and the retrograde conditions of employment to which he and they had had to adjust themselves. He came of a stock that had owned a cottage and had possessed certain rights of pasturage and a share in the commonland, which had served to supplement wages and had enabled the families to live in a certain degree of comfort. By the passing of the Enclosure Acts these small-holdings were taken out of the hands of the peasant-owners and were given over to swell the acres already held by land-owners and tenant-farmers. The labourers were thus entirely dependent on their wages as their means of subsistence. This changed the old order of things: it meant that the distance between their employers and themselves had increased both socially and financially. Whereas in the old days the farmers had been but little removed from themselves in social status, the men were now 'reduced to a servile dependence on their mercy'.

The days were passing when the farm men took their place at the farmer's table to share the mid-day meal: when, after work was done in the dairy and kitchen, farmer's wife and serving maid would take up their spinning or knitting and enjoy a gossip over the doings of the village—a subject in which both would be interested. The position of man working for man was an altogether different one now that man worked for a master. It meant that sympathies were alienated and that community of interests was destroyed. Previously the labourers had been farming jacks-of-all-trades—general farm-workers. Now, with the increase in the size of the farms and in the amount of stock kept, labour was much more specialized. The 'man who looked after the cows', but who took a turn with the plough, or hedged and ditched between milking hours, now became the cowman and that solely. This change may have effected an increase of efficiency, but it certainly caused a loss of interest by the workmen in the general welfare of the farm itself. To add to the prevailing discontent and suspicion, experiments in the use of agricultural machinery were being tried and had involved a reduction of labour where successful. This had thrown many hands out of work and revolts had resulted.

The farmers' concern for their employees seems to have decreased in degree as their importance in position increased in extent; the wages they paid were still preposterously low. The poor could seldom afford to buy meat or butter, and even potatoes were a luxury. The normal food of a cottager's family was dry bread, horse-beans, a poor quality of cheese, and 'roots'—turnips, swedes and so forth. In most of the southern counties by 1834 agitations by the labourers had induced the farmers to pay a minimum wage of 10s. a week to their work-people, but in Dorset all such efforts had been unsuccessful and the rate of pay per week was still 7s. The poverty and misery that these conditions entailed can only dimly be imagined, but it is not difficult to comprehend the universal gloom that had spread itself like a cloud over agricultural life.

This, in brief, was the position as George Loveless viewed it, and his sturdy independence was roused to revolt at the survey. Individual action had been unavailing; corporate bargaining for better conditions must now be essayed. The first step he took was one of peaceful persuasion. He laid the case before Mr. William Morton Pitt, of Kingston, who advised a meeting in Dorchester between an equal number of representatives of the farmers and labourers. This meeting took place in the County Hall, presided over by Mr. James Frampton, a local Justice of the Peace, who, as future events proved, could not be considered exactly impartial in the matter. Be that as it may, the meeting was a failure, and George Loveless returned to Tolpuddle disconsolate. He had also enlisted the support of the local vicar—Dr. Warren—who consented to act as a deputation to the local farmers, to demand a promise that they would pay a minimum weekly wage of 10s. to their workers. The farmers relented at the time, but procrastinated from week to week and finally failed to put their promise into effect. Dr. Warren seems to have played a craven part in this affair, for when asked to approach the farmers again to demand the substantiation of their promises, he refused to take further action.

Negotiations had failed. George Loveless did not contemplate coercion by rick-burning, property-destroying or disorders of such kind, but he now turned to another method of approach which had been pursued in other districts and in other trades.

Trade unions were then being formed in many industries and manufactories, but up to that time little had been done by such a method of combination amongst agricultural labourers. In 1833, Loveless applied to the central body, which afterwards became the Grand National Consolidated Trades Union, for advice and help in forming a union, and with this end in view, two delegates were sent down to interview him and his associates. The Union was formed on December 9th of the same year, and the Grand Lodge of Tolpuddle of the Agricultural Labourers Friendly Society was duly inaugurated, with all the strange ceremony and initiation rites that the trade unions required in those days. New members were blindfolded and after a short religious service—the reading of a prayer or two and the singing of a hymn—they were made to swear on oath loyalty to the union and its objects, and that they would protect and stand by their fellow-members. Those who joined were required to pay one shilling on admission and a subscription of a penny a week. Secrecy was enjoined on all: members were not allowed to inform their wives or families that they were in any way connected with the union. The rôle of conspirator in no way suited the candid and honest-natured George Loveless, but in some places such injustice and hardship had followed on the exposure of members' names, that concealment was advocated.

The Union grew in numbers and influence, not only in Tolpuddle, but in the neighbouring districts. As it was bound to do sooner or later, the knowledge of its formation became common property: you might as well expect a sieve to hold water as a village to keep a secret. When the landowners and farmers heard of it they became alarmed. They read their newspapers, and were well aware of the effect that these unions were producing in other parts of the country, and how wage concessions were being granted as a result of powerful trade and labour combinations. They took counsel amongst themselves as to the best steps to take in defence, and proceeded to collect evidence and the names of the union leaders. Their attitude seems superlatively foolish and short-sighted. Had lust of wealth and pride of newly-won position blinded them to the inhumanity of their conduct? Were they so dull that they could not foresee the possible consequences of the line that they were taking? They might with advantage have learned a parable from their own farm-yards—that a dog tethered by a short leash becomes suspicious, surly-tempered and dangerous; but a dog well-treated and at liberty will serve his master the more faithfully by reason of his freedom.

The farmers took their first active step by reporting the fact of the Union to the local magistrates, who were themselves interested parties as landowners. One can imagine how the matter soon became a topic of conversation at the local dinner parties and at the cattle-pens on market days. Such perplexity as there was: such blusterings, such denunciations! What speculations as to the immediate outcome of the labourers' action! What gloomy prognostications as to the future of the country, and the speed with which it was going to the dogs! Mr. James Frampton of Moreton Hall was most exasperated. He had thought that the meeting in Dorchester had shown these men how unwarrantable had been their demands, how impossible of fulfilment, but, as they had plainly not learnt their lesson, he was determined to deal with the situation by drastic measures. This was not the first time that he had come into collision with the labourers. In 1830, throughout the county, a demand had been made for an increase in the rate of wages; on the refusal of the farmers, risings in different areas had resulted. Mr. Frampton had been foremost in opposition to the labourers and had sworn in special constables, and at Bere Regis 'had harangued the people and argued with them on the impropriety of their conduct, refusing to concede to their demands whilst asked with menaces'. The rioters had replied by threatening to besiege Moreton Hall, and were only prevented from burning it down by the constant vigilance of the household, and the Dorset Militia, who patrolled the estate at night-time.

Mr. Frampton now applied to Lord Digby, the Lord Lieutenant of the county, and he in his turn wrote to Lord Melbourne, the Whig Home Secretary at the time, reporting the growth of these combinations 'which were of a dangerous and alarming kind', and asking for instructions in dealing with the instigators. No doubt Lord Melbourne sighed on the receipt of this letter. The Government was being pestered from all quarters of the industrial world to pass some legislative measure against the trade union movement. The Acts against Combinations of Workmen had been repealed in 1825, and since then the unions had pursued an aggressive policy so successfully that Lord Melbourne had been obliged to consider the matter seriously. He had instructed Mr. Nassau Senior, Professor of Political Economy at Oxford, to prepare a report for the Cabinet on the existing situation with suggestions for combating the effects of the unions and for limiting their influence. The report when it came out was too drastic in its repressive recommendations, to be adopted by a Whig Government with its avowed ideal of protecting the constitution and liberties of the country. The Government had therefore no policy formed, and Lord Melbourne had no advice to offer Lord Digby. He did suggest, however, that 'in cases of this description suitable provisions relative to the administration of secret oaths had been frequently resorted to with advantage'. James Frampton accepted this hint with alacrity. He and his fellow magistrates put it into effect by publishing a Proclamation ordering the men to disband their union, as such unions, which bound members by the administration of secret oaths, were illegal. The Proclamation ran thus:

CAUTION

Whereas it has been represented to us from several quarters that mischievous and designing Persons have been for some time past, endeavouring to induce, and have induced, many Labourers in various Parishes in this County, to attend Meetings, and to enter into illegal Societies and Unions, to which they bind themselves by unlawful oaths, administered secretly by Persons concealed, who artfully deceive the ignorant and unwary,—We, the undersigned Justices think it our duty to give this PUBLIC NOTICE and CAUTION that all Persons may know the danger they incur by entering into such Societies.

Any Person who shall become a member of such a Society, or assent to any Test or Declaration not authorized by Law—
Any Person who shall administer, or be present at, or consenting to the administering or taking any Unlawful Oath, or who shall cause such Oath to be administered, altho' not actually present at the time—
Any Person who shall not reveal or discover any Illegal Oath which may have been administered, or any Illegal Act done or to be done—
Any Person who shall induce, or endeavour to persuade any other Person to become a Member of such Societies,

will become

GUILTY OF Felony

and be Liable to be

TRANSPORTED FOR SEVEN YEARS.

Any Person who shall be compelled to take such an oath, unless he shall declare the same within four days, together with the whole of what he shall know touching the same, will be liable to the same penalty.

The notice was printed on the front page of the *Dorset County Chronicle* on February 20th, 1833; it was also posted in conspicuous places in

Tolpuddle and the surrounding villages two days later. It caught the eye of George Loveless, who put a copy of it into his pocket to investigate at leisure. At first sight it looked to be a bombshell, but the legal position had to be examined. Were the magistrates within their rights in publishing such an edict? Anyway, the matter must wait till such times as a meeting with the other union men could be arranged.

Events moved too speedily, however: there was no time for debate. On February 24th, very early in the morning, the Dorchester Constable made his appearance in Tolpuddle with warrants for the arrest of six of the villagers known to be connected with the union, and they were marched off to Dorchester gaol. What excitement must have pervaded Tolpuddle! The arrested men were probably only surprised and indignant; their consciences were clear. No time had been allowed for the dissolution of the union, even had the leaders been convinced of the need for such an action. Unions such as theirs had been organized all over the country and under the same conditions, and it would create an impossible situation if all were found to be illegal and if all union leaders and members were to be arrested! Some such comforting reflections, no doubt, passed through George Loveless's mind, as he traversed the seven miles to the County town. There they were paraded before James Frampton, who, as the only magistrate on the bench that day, heard the case against the prisoners and committed them to prison. Later on, they appeared before a full bench of magistrates, when sufficient evidence was produced, according to the Justices, to incriminate them all and they were sentenced to await trial at the forthcoming Assizes.

When in prison, George Loveless was interviewed by a local solicitor, presumably with the object of extracting information concerning the union and other unknown members. He baffled the lawyer by his unabashed demeanour and his critical attitude towards the procedure pursued by the magistrates. He maintained that there was nothing unlawful in forming a union; that insufficient time had elapsed between the publication of the Proclamation and the arrest, for him to have taken any action; and that as for the charge that unlawful oaths had been administered, in what Society—Freemasons, Oddfellows and the like—were oaths not so administered? He would give no information against other members of the union, needless to say, and altogether the interview went badly for the representative of the Law.

The suspense of the weeks that followed must have been hard alike for the prisoners, their families, and the neighbourhood generally. The patience and courage of the men in gaol were sorely tried by their confinement alongside thieves, poachers, miscreants of all descriptions, whose coarse language, degrading habits, and licentious talk, must have disgusted the decent and God-fearing Methodists. The consternation of the labouring class throughout the district can be imagined. The surrounding counties had used the weapon of trade unionism to obtain their demands, and had been successful. Were the men of Dorset to be deprived of the only means that they knew of insisting on better conditions and a stabilized living wage in return for their labour? They had been so sanguine of the results of this effort at combination and confident of its success. Now the pall of frustration was thrown over the dead bones of hope: it was a grim spectre which stalked from village to village. The action of the farmers and magistrates exaggerated ten-fold the distrust and hostility between themselves and their work-people, and the relations between Church and Nonconformity became further strained. Rightly or wrongly, the latter considered that the Church sided with reactionary Toryism and capitalism, and that its attitude towards the acute labour questions of the day ill-accorded with the Christianity it taught. There was a suspicion that it was the type of the prisoners' religion that caused the magistrates to be so particularly relentless: and this suspicion became a certainty when the story of the prison chaplain's interview with the prisoners became known. He upbraided them for the conduct which had brought them to their present plight, without inquiring into the cause of their discontent. It was not the best way to approach men already sore with a sense of injustice and the ignominy of their position.

The Assizes were to be held in Dorchester in the following March. One must realize at the outset that the stage on which the drama was to be played was set in a larger theatre than that of a Dorchester Assize Court. The principal players were not merely six Dorset labourers and their betrayers, but puppets under the direction of political intrigue, with Judge Williams as the principal showman. He was a friend of Lord Melbourne and a well-known supporter of the Whig party. He had been a successful barrister on the

Northern Circuit and, owing to a vacancy on the Judicial Bench, had been appointed to a Judgeship, and was now being sent to Dorchester to hold his first Assize. He appears to have been a good man at his job, popular on Bench and Bar and sincere in the interpretation of his legal duties. It is only to be presumed that, in the case before us, his critical judgment was subordinated to his desire to do his party a service. As we have already observed, Lord Melbourne was in a cleft stick in his position with regard to trade unionism. He could hardly fight it on a political field: might he perhaps conduct a legal sortie against it? Judge Williams undertook to see what could be done in Dorset.

The excitement in Dorchester on March 18th, the day of the Assizes, was intense, and the court was crowded with representatives from all classes of the community. The Grand Jury, under the foremanship of the Hon. William Ponsonby, returned a True Bill against the prisoners and the trial was proceeded with. The charge preferred against them was, in simple language, that 'of administering an unlawful oath' according to the 'Unlawful Oaths Act'. This Act had been passed in 1797 to deal specifically with the Mutiny of the Nore, but it had actually never been repealed.

The chief evidence that could be produced for the Prosecution was given by two labourers, John Lark and Edward Legg, who admitted having been at a meeting with the prisoners, where all present swore on oath their fealty to the union and its objects. They described the proceeding rather vaguely—how they had been blindfolded, and how, after a short reading which they had not understood, they all knelt down and an oath was administered to them. They were made to kiss a book, 'which looked like a Bible', and a picture of a skeleton with skull and cross-bones was shown to them. Other evidence chiefly to prove the complicity of George Loveless, was supplied by a woman whose husband was a painter. Loveless, she declared, had come to her with instructions for her husband to paint a figure representing 'Death' and another of a skeleton—both to be painted on wood and to be 'six foot high'. A paper had also been found in the house of Loveless, which appeared to contain the rules of the Society of Labourers in general, and those applicable to the local branch in particular. A copy of the magistrates' proclamation had also been found in his pocket.

The Counsel for the prisoners urged in defence the excellent character borne by them all. He argued that administration of oaths had always been employed in the trade union organization, that no legal exception had been taken to it before, and that such oaths were common in many other secret societies. He contended that the law under which they were being indicted had only legislated for particular cases of mutiny and sedition in His Majesty's Forces, and did not apply to civil cases. Finally, he pointed out that no intimidation or threats had been used towards the farmers in consequence of the union, a fact which should certainly be taken into consideration.

The Judge summed up, dwelling at length on the enormity of trifling with oaths and the cruelty of forcing men out of their scanty earnings to make to trade union funds, 'such a large and ample contribution as would not be endured by any class of men to the constituted authorities of the Country or the maintenance of the Government itself'. He directed the jury to find the prisoners guilty if they were satisfied that an unlawful oath had been administered, and is said to have concluded his address with the words:—'If these men had been allowed to go on with their wicked plans they would have destroyed property. If you do not find them guilty you will forfeit the goodwill and confidence of the members of the Grand Jury.' He then gave the prisoners a chance to state their case. George Loveless was the spokesman, and began a spirited defence—possibly too much in the style of a Methodist 'ranter'—for Judge Williams soon stopped the discourse and bade him confine what he had to say to a written statement. Loveless did this with astonishing dispatch, and the result was handed to the judge to be read aloud:—'We were uniting to preserve ourselves, our wives and our children from utter degradation and starvation. We have injured no man's reputation, character, person, or property.' So ran his statement, which was remarkable alike for its simplicity as for its substance, and was moreover a poignant appeal for a merciful judgment. Their wrongs were real: their wounds ran deep. Was that no excuse for what at worst was only an error of organization?

Amidst a hushed silence, the jury left the court to consider their verdict. The judge had plainly conveyed in his address his opinion as to the culpability of the prisoners. For the first time since their arrest, George Loveless and his fellows, dazed and bewildered by the events of the day and the long hours in Court, contemplated the possibility that the case might go against them.

It was a slow dawning to slow country minds, but the light was not the less piercing when it broke through. Those present in the court were no less awestruck. Many of them, but for the grace of God, might have been in the prisoners' dock. Possibly even the magistrates and farmers felt some qualms of conscience as to their responsibility in the affair, and glanced shamefacedly round on their fellow-conspirators.

The jury was absent five minutes only; and returned to deliver the verdict of 'guilty'. Little choice had been left them after the definite summing up of the judge.

Two days later the judge was again in court to deliver the sentence, which was seven years transportation for all six prisoners. 'The object of all legal punishment is not altogether with the view of operating on the offenders themselves, it is also for the sake of offering an example and a warning,' spoke the judge. 'I am not sentencing you for any crime you have committed or that it could be proved that you were about to commit, but as an example to the working-classes of this country.' The verdict on the Tolpuddle Martyrs might be correct according to the strict letter of the law, but surely the sentence could never be defended on any grounds whatever? On the following day, *The Times* reported the proceeding and commented thus:—'This sentence as regards the poor deluded men who are the object of it, seems to us too severe; but it may be useful if it spreads alarm among those more acute and powerful disturbers of the town populations throughout England.' The very opposite occurred. True, the use of the 'secret oaths' in the admission of new members was abolished, but trade unionism took strides forward as a result of the interest and indignation aroused in the Dorchester trial.

The men were sent down in chains to Portsmouth the same week. There they were taken on one of the convict hulks and were put to work with the chain-gang on the Gun Wharf, alongside all the criminals likewise awaiting transportation. Their situation can be better imagined than described. So great was the scandal of the mixing and treatment of the prisoners that it was not many years later that the punishment of transportation to Australia was abolished.

Thus another step was cut in the rock that Labour sought to scale in its ascent towards 'Liberty to Organize'. If a few lives were chipped in the hewing, only so much the more would the way be valued by those who followed the path.

No cause can be won without sacrifice; no martyrs' crown without suffering. Let trade unionism see to it that it is worthy of the blood and tears that have been shed in its service.

CHAPTER IV

THE YEARS OF MARTYRDOM

IT is impossible to imagine what misery the martyrs suffered during the six weeks that they lived in the convict hulks at Portsmouth. If three weeks spent in the company of typical habitués of a country-town lock-up had wellnigh sickened them, the close contact with some of the very worst criminals of the day must have been overwhelming in its horror. What must these new conditions have meant to countrymen accustomed to the clean air of clover-fields and honeysuckled lanes; accustomed to daily tramps from ploughfield to byre, from sheepfold to stackyard with the slow-moving beasts of the farm, to whose intelligence they had learnt to adapt themselves, whose serenity they had learnt to emulate? The stench of unclean, unhealthy humanity, the shackled limbs, the companionship of men whose speech and jests were coarse and licentious, whose very souls were sodden with evil—all this must have revolted the homely, simple labourers. Moreover, they were bewildered; the busy stir of the seaport town and the crowded, riotous life in the hulks was different from anything that they had hitherto experienced. They were anxious about their homes and families. What did their wives and mothers know of their present plight? How were they being supported? Doubtless the men of Tolpuddle knew that neighbours would rally round; they could trust in that divine spirit of generosity which the very poor bear towards one another. God knows seven shillings was little enough on which to feed and clothe one family: it was manifestly impossible for it to satisfy any extra mouths. Neighbours might have the will to help, but had they the means?

One wonders how much a sense of injustice rankled in the hearts of these men, or whether the consciousness of their martyrdom in the cause of freedom was an exaltation which lifted them above their sordid surroundings. Possibly having been reared to the vagaries and uncertainties of farming life they accepted each day as it came and looked neither far behind nor too far ahead. They were inured to disappointments: to seeing the rain smashing down day after day on a promising harvest: to watching—impotent and helpless—the best ploughing horse stricken down with fatal horse-sickness: to waiting in vain for that blessed spring rain which would swell the roots and stimulate the pasture.

The conditions on the convict-ship *William Metcalf* seem to have been brutal and degrading. For fourteen weeks the convicts were only allowed four hours of each day on deck. Their sleeping berths were so crowded that many of them could never lie at full length to take proper rest.

George Loveless was landed at Hobart on September 9th. There he was brought before the magistrates and the Governor, who each in turn questioned him searchingly on his work for the trade unions. They seem to have been suspicious and hostile, but eventually the obvious sincerity and candour of Loveless won him some measure of favour with the Governor. For a time he worked on the making of new roads with the chain-gang. This meant long hours of labour in the grilling sun, chained to a convict on either side, the irons of the fetters chafing their sweating flesh. The overseers seem to have been brutal men, flogging the prisoners if they did but raise their heads for a moment from their toil. No doubt their own nerves were frayed by long hours in the heat, and their feelings blunted by constant association with hardened criminals, by whom sharp commands and the whip's lash would be the only language understood.

After some months, by the special instructions of the Governor, Loveless was sent to work on the Government Farm. Conditions here were somewhat better. It is true that the sleeping quarters were cramped and barely weather-proof, and the food was so scanty and of such poor quality that complaints thereon were sent to England, which eventually effected some improvement in the commissariat; but to Loveless the new position must have been welcome indeed. He was at last free from the chains which bound convict to convict: he was on farm work to which he had been bred and which he loved. He was appointed stock-man on the farm; it was a heavy job of work for one man, but he did not fear labour. Reports of his character and competence were sent again and again to the Governor, and only once was he brought up before the magistrates for neglect of duty. It was proved, however, to the magistrates' satisfaction that George had had more to perform on a particular occasion than any one man could possibly accomplish, and he was sent back to his job without any reflection on his character as a worker. When he had been in Tasmania for over twelve months, it was suggested to Loveless that he should send for his wife and family. This he refused to do as long as he was a prisoner. The authorities were annoyed with his attitude until finally, after repeated requests on their part, he consented, and wrote home to Mrs. Loveless asking her to come out to him.

Meanwhile the other martyrs, who had been sent on to Sydney, were existing in circumstances of even greater hardship.

James Loveless had much the same tale to relate as his brother. He also worked in chains on the roads, was threatened with floggings, was housed and fed disgracefully. James Brine, after working on the roads likewise, was sent to work on a farm about fifty miles inland. He set out to walk the distance and was robbed on the way by bushrangers, who stole his boots, and the bed, blanket and shilling that had been given him for the journey. He arrived at his destination in a starved and miserable condition, his bare feet bleeding. His state, however, induced no kindly commiseration in his employer, and he was put immediately to work on digging post-holes for fences without even a meal to revive him. No new boots seem to have been forthcoming, and we are told that Brine worked for six months, digging post-holes in rough ground in his bare feet, his only protection being an old piece of hoop-iron bent and tied to his foot to take the pressure of the spade. He slept on the ground; had no change of clothing, only the old convict suit in which he had left England. Such inhumanity on the part of any man seems impossible to credit in these soft days. Hard times bred harsh men, and the prevailing conditions of existence were not conducive to easy terms for labour, but the limit of cruelty must surely have been reached in Brine's case.

The Standfields were separated from one another for a time—a great grief to John, who pined to know how his old father was faring. John was sent to work on a farm a hundred and fifty miles up-country from Sydney, and soon afterwards heard by chance that his father was employed as shepherd on a neighbouring farm. The old man had charge of five hundred or more sheep, which had to be driven daily through the bush from farm to pasture and back again. It was no easy job guarding a flock of such dimensions, and bringing it intact, in every kind of weather, through the thick scrub where many dangers lurked. The loss of a sheep meant a flogging, the dread of which was a constant nightmare to the old man. The living conditions were bad. Each day, after sundown, he had to walk a distance of four miles to draw his daily rations: the shed where he slept was only just large enough to permit his lying at full length, and he was provided with but one blanket as a covering.

In January, 1838, both Standfields were summoned to appear before the magistrates of Maitland. There they were relegated to the lock-up, where they were imprisoned for three days, existing on bread and water, and with neither bed nor blanket on which to sleep. Fetters were then fastened on them and they were chained to eight convicts and sent by steam-boat to Newcastle and thence to Sydney—a journey of a hundred and fifty miles. The passage was particularly rough, and all the prisoners were sea-sick; scarcely any food was served out to them, and they were never released from the burden of the handcuffs during the whole journey. The ensuing ten days were no more comfortable: the Standfields seem to have been shifted from one Sydney gaol to another; they were nearly starved, and provided with neither bed nor bedding. Moreover, they were chained to criminals of the worst description—verily an example of the lamb and the lion lying down together! After a period of a week or ten days, the father and son were separated from their companions and sent back to a sheep-farm near Maitland, where they worked for the remainder of their time in Australia.

This tale of the Standfields is very moving. One can imagine the distress of John at seeing the treatment meted out to his father. The poor old man tried valiantly to make light of his troubles and keep up an appearance of cheer before his son. Did England know to what she was committing her sons when she sent them to Botany Bay? These same sons may have committed dastardly crimes, violated laws and caused their parent expense and trouble, but that she should remain unheeding, unmoved by the terrible tales that travelled back to her across the water bids one pause and ponder the patience of the labouring classes who were the chief victims of the criminal injustice and neglect of the Mother Country. Correction should never spell cruelty: punishment never barbarity.

Of James Hammett we hear little that is authentic, but probably his existence followed a no more flowery path than that of his friends. He was sold for £1 to a farmer living four hundred miles from Sydney, and was dispatched thither to find his way as best he might. He, like Brine, was presented with an outfit consisting of a bed, blanket, and a shilling, and rations to last him twenty-two days. Of his journey he tells us nothing, but it requires little imagination to picture the privations of such a pilgrimage. How he arrived at his destination in a practically uncharted country passes understanding. Small wonder that many convicts sent off on such journeys never attempted to undertake them, but joined the bands of bushrangers that were a menace to the country and a terror to the inland population. James Hammett was not one to be deflected from his purpose: he set out to reach a given point, there he arrived, and there he worked on a sheep-run for nearly four years. Of all the Dorset martyrs his sacrifice was the most selfless, as there is good reason to believe that he had had nothing to do with the trade union, but had been arrested in mistake for a brother who was a member. James was a true son of Dorset soil—patient, inarticulate, enduring. Of his sufferings or his emotions he volunteered nothing, and kept silence, even when pressed to tell his tale on his arrival home. History does not reveal the cause of his reticence, but we may well imagine that a retailing of the hardships which he had undergone would have added poignancy to the already deep remorse of the brother whose place he had taken.

Meanwhile in England agitation for the release of the martyrs increased as the knowledge of their conviction and sentence spread. In a surprisingly short time we hear of Members of Parliament presenting petitions from their constituents, pleading for the release and return of the prisoners. As early as March 26th—barely a week after the trial—the first petition was presented in the Commons by the member for Oxford. Again on April 14th, 16th and 18th, petitions came up from Cheltenham, Hull, Yeovil, Gomersal, Liverpool and Leeds, representing as may be realized every class of worker. By the end of that month, a torrent of protest had flowed in from the manufacturing centres until it was estimated that 80,000 names had been signed to petitions from all over the country. Pleas put forth were that the administration of secret oaths was a common part of the proceedings in many societies and no legal action had been taken before; that the labourers were acting in ignorance that they were breaking any law of the land when they formed their union according to customary trade union ceremony; that far milder sentences had been passed oftentimes on more serious crimes. A display of mercy was urged by J. A. Roebuck in his pamphlet entitled *The Dorchester Labourers*, on the grounds of the debt the country owed the labouring countrymen for their services in its defence. 'Read any of the histories of our wars and they will speak of the patience, the fortitude and the perseverance of the English soldier.' The Government remained static and aloof amidst the turmoil that boiled and seethed round it, and all through April and the early days of May reiterated (without truth) that the prisoners had already sailed.

On April 21st, the Grand National Consolidated Trades Union arranged a demonstration in London with the object of soliciting the King's pardon on behalf of the prisoners. It was organized by Robert Owen, the well-known social reformer, and he was partnered by the Rev. Arthur Wade, Vicar of S. Nicholas', Warwick. When these two men realized the excitement that the projected demonstration was likely to arouse, they determined that the utmost care should be exercised in preserving dignity and discipline in the procession, so that the Government should have no rightful cause to complain that riots and disorders had resulted. The Copenhagen Fields near King's Cross had been hired for the occasion, and there the demonstrators assembled. It was an immense procession, numbering some thirty or forty thousand, composed of representatives from trade unions all over England, and thousands of sympathizers, Wesleyans, Churchmen, Whigs and Tories, who all saw in the transportation of the martyrs, not merely an example of political jobbery, but a deliberate attack on the freedom of Englishmen, and a degradation of British justice and prestige. The procession marched in perfect order by way of the Tottenham Court Road, Oxford Street, Regent Street, to Whitehall. Robert Owen and Dr. Wade, both on horseback, the latter arrayed in full canonicals with his hood as a Doctor of Divinity, directed the crowds. Lord Melbourne refused to receive a deputation from the demonstrators, but consented to hand on a petition from them—if signed and properly authenticated—to the King for his perusal. This petition, signed with half a million names, was duly presented to King William three days later. The procession dispersed on Kennington Common towards the close of the day, having kept perfect order and with no display of bad feeling throughout—which spoke well for the strength of Owen's influence and the moderation and restraint of the trade union organizers. Demonstrations had also been held in other centres, notably on Newcastle Moor, where 10,000 men assembled to demand the release of the prisoners. Many of the protests came from Whig supporters, who felt that the Government had grossly mismanaged the affair. It had sacrificed party principles to the desire of propping up a tottering ministry by an illusory show of strength and determination which was exceedingly ill-advised.

By August, 1834, the Grand National Consolidated Trades Union had ceased to exist, but agitation for the release of the prisoners still continued. The 'Dorchester Labourers Committee' was formed to keep alive the agitation and a fund in connection therewith was opened, with Richard Hartwell as its treasurer. The fund was well supported by sympathizers of every class and creed, and it did much to relieve the want and privations of the martyrs' families in Tolpuddle, who meanwhile had been faring badly. The James Hammetts had been turned out of their cottage; his old mother had been dispatched to the workhouse, while his wife and sister found refuge with his brother John, whose cottage was small and already full to overflowing. When the notice came to vacate their cottages, the Lovelesses and Standfields showed some spirit of resistance and both families had to be forcibly evicted by the bailiff before they would quit. Neighbours housed the forlorn families somehow, but the problem of feeding was only solved by the whole village being brought nearer than ever before to the brink of starvation.

It was not until the next year, 1835, that public expostulations received much attention. Thomas Wakley then stepped into the picture. He was the Member for Finsbury, a doctor of medicine, and an energetic, warm-hearted man, zealous in the cause of improving conditions for the poor. He had travelled down to Tolpuddle to interview the friends and relations of the martyrs, and had returned to London deeply moved and impressed by all that he had seen and heard. In June, 1835, he introduced the subject in the Commons, pleading that an address might be presented to the King, asking his pardon for the Dorchester labourers. In an impressive speech, he painted a vivid background to the picture that he wished to set before his fellow-members, giving details of the poverty that existed in the country areas generally and in Dorset in particular. He described his visit to Tolpuddle and quoted extracts from letters received by Mrs. Loveless from her husband to bear witness to the spirit in which he was sustaining his exile. In one letter he wrote:

> I thank you, my dear wife, for the consideration that you have ever paid me, and you may safely rely upon it that as long as I live, it will be my constant endeavour to return that kindness in every possible way. I shall never forget the promise made at the Altar: and though we may part awhile, I shall consider myself under the same obligations as though being in your immediate presence.

Again:

> Be satisfied, my dear Betsy, on my account. Depend upon it, it will work together for good and we shall yet rejoice together. I hope you will pay particular attention to the moral and spiritual interests of the children. Don't send me any money to distress yourself: I shall do well, for He who is the Lord of the winds and waves will be my support in life and death.

These sentiments were not those of a rabid revolutionary or an unbalanced labour agitator; there was no mention of the hardships or ill-treatment that he was enduring: no denunciations against the country of his martyrdom, or word in recrimination of the men who had sent him there. Dr. Wakley then proceeded to sketch in the middle distance of his picture the trial and the events which followed it. He declared that the men were ignorant that any crime was being committed in organizing efforts at combination, and drew attention to their determination that no disorder should accrue as a result of their federation. In conclusion, he pleaded in forceful terms that for the sake of the good name of British justice, the King's pardon should be entreated, and that their return should immediately be ordered.

Lord John Russell spoke in opposition: he considered that if remission of the sentence were allowed, it would 'impair the influence which that great institution, trial by judge and jury, ought to have in this country'. He spoke of the havoc to industry and capital which would result if the workers were permitted to make bargains with their employers as to the wages they were entitled to receive. The motion was put to the House and lost by three hundred and eight votes to eighty-two, but Wakley was undismayed and continued his indefatigable efforts to secure pardon and release for the Tolpuddle men. Nearly a year later, in March, 1836, he again brought up the subject in Parliament, whereupon Lord John Russell announced (no doubt with some satisfaction that a troublesome and somewhat smutty page of history had finally been turned over) that the King's pardon had been procured, and the return of the Martyrs was merely a matter of time.

Postal communication with Australia was slow in those days, and what with the delay caused in this way and with the reluctance of the Australian officials to inform the prisoners of their free pardon it was not until twelve months later that George Loveless returned to England. He had been delayed by the fact that he had, at the instance of the Tasmanian Government, suggested to his wife that she should come out to him. Naturally, he had to be assured that she had not started on her journey before he left the country. He was in possession of the address of his nephew, John Standfield and to him he wrote, announcing the news of their pardon and advising the best methods of securing the free passages home that were part of the terms of release. On receipt of this letter, John wrote to his other uncle, James Loveless, begging him to make application for all three of them. At length, the passages were granted and these three, in company with James Brine, sailed for home on September 11th, 1837, arriving at

Plymouth the following March. James Hammett, unlucky as ever, heard nothing of the bestowal of the free pardon for some months, and only by chance then, did he read the fact in an old newspaper. He lost no time in demanding his release, but even so it was August, 1838, before he set foot in England. The Government had ordered that first-class passages should be supplied to the Martyrs for their return journey; these were not forthcoming, but probably the men were in no mood to cavil at what to them was a matter of small inconvenience.

Man can have no conception of the value he sets on his liberty, until he is deprived of it. After four years, these men were free—free from the physical gall of chains and handcuffs: from the presence of degrading associates: from the humiliation of exposure to undeserved insult and suspicion: free to enjoy the marvels of land and sea through which they were travelling. Vision of the immensity, the wonder, and the majesty of the universe helps man to realize his own comparative insignificance; and perhaps for the Martyrs the sight of vast spaces of sea and sky did something to reduce to their proper proportions the ill-usage, the injustice and the suffering of the last few years.

On arrival in England, they were acclaimed and welcomed by sympathizers in Plymouth and elsewhere. Of their reception in Tolpuddle one may not write, though probably a stranger homecoming has never been experienced; the sweetness of reunion was so mingled with the bitterness of the tale each had to reveal.

James Hammett was the only one of the six to remain in Tolpuddle. There he lived and worked until he lost his sight, when—independent as ever—he departed to the workhouse to end his days there, rather than be a burden on his family. The remaining five migrated to Essex, where they were set up in farms purchased for them by the 'Dorchester Labourers' Fund'. After two years, however, they all left Essex and England and settled in Canada. The motives which prompted this step can only be surmised. Perhaps to them agricultural life in England seemed on too small a scale after their taste of the wide spaces of Australia. Perhaps they felt the necessity of withdrawal to some place where the echo of their imprisonment would not reach them. In England there were too many reminders of a past which had better be submerged. None of them had sought for fame or glory in this life or set out to make history, but notoriety had been thrust upon them. Now they required that they might sink back into that obscurity from which they fain would never have emerged. There may also have been a religious impulse to urge them to the move. Since the sixteenth century there had always been a strong Puritan element in Dorset and many Dorchester families had emigrated to America in the early days of colonization. In the porch of St. Peter's Church, Dorchester, a tablet commemorates a former rector who 'greatly set forward the migration to the Massachusett Bay colony, where his name lives in unfading remembrance'. Perhaps this tradition attracted Loveless, and he and his friends set off to Canada to enjoy a greater religious freedom than that which had been vouchsafed them in England.

In 1912, a fund was raised through the energies of a Dorset County official and a Memorial Arch was erected over the gateway leading to the little Methodist Chapel in Tolpuddle which replaced the old barn where Loveless once preached. That is the only memorial in stone raised to the memory of the Martyrs, but it is to be hoped that the Centenary will awaken in the national memory the need for a more worthy recognition than has heretofore been accorded them.

It may not come amiss before the close of this

chapter to record shortly the immediate outcome of the Tolpuddle tragedy. It had an effect on three spheres of influence, the agricultural labouring class, the trade union movement, and the Wesleyan Methodists.

The village labourers were temporarily aroused from the apathy which had fallen on them after their brief and sporadic revolt at the Enclosure Acts. This further example of the farmers' hostility was cast into the stew-pot of their grievances, which had been simmering for years, and now boiled over into an expressed bitterness of spirit and an active sympathy with the Tolpuddle victims. The loyalty which exists between men of like trade is of still stauncher quality among those who bear the love of the land in common. Unfortunately, the labourers soon seem to have been intimidated, and relaxed their efforts at combination. Thus to many the Martyrs' sacrifice seemed a vain one. But was it? George Loveless, like his fellow martyrs, loved the land upon which he worked. The farm labourers of that time were only removed by one generation from the peasants who had owned the land they worked on, and had inherited from their forebears the pride and love of it which amounted almost to a passion in their lives. Since the passing of the Enclosure Acts the right of possession had been denied them, but they still loved the land for its own sake, and George Loveless and others of his kind were dumbly resentful that the land they loved so well should be exploited for unworthy ends and be the cause of so much misery to those who laboured for it. The land was not tyrannical: but the farmers, who were reducing the lives of their hirelings to slavery, might be considered so. George Loveless and his fellows had been denied the right of pride in possession: they now fought for the right of freedom in service.

To the trade union organizers and labour agitators, the Tolpuddle tale of hardship and injustice was a tempting dish of propaganda to serve up to the discontented workers of the day. It was easy to inflame the imagination of the most slow-witted with this story of the tyranny of the ruling classes, who sought to force subjection on their work-people and who countenanced the perversion of the law to this end. Here again, the trade union movement was inclined to deem the Tolpuddle efforts to organize combination a failure, because as a result the Agricultural Labourers Union lost heart and was soon afterwards dissolved. But succeeding generations of trade unionists acknowledge gratefully the stimulation that the event contributed to the movement.

The life of the Church had been reduced to a low ebb in the early years of the nineteenth century, and was especially dead in country districts. But man's need for a religion is innate and Wesley's teaching was winning followers wherever it was preached. Once again, it was a case of the common people who heard gladly. It was mainly a religion of Christian ethics based on a study of Christ's life and teaching, and it was to a great extent—at any rate in those early years—divorced from social and political considerations of the age. Many good Methodists, who might have remained unmoved by the waves of labour unrest that were passing over the country, became now perturbed at this intrusion of politics into the sphere of their religious beliefs. It was not because he was a Methodist preacher that George Loveless took the action that he did. Because he believed in the Fatherhood of God, he believed also in the brotherhood of man, and he sought to establish it in deed as well as in word. Social station or riches meant little to a man who was burning with the zeal of his religion, which taught him that love of God and neighbour was the one essential for the only aristocracy worthy of consideration. If some members of the community mistook their privileges and sought by the power of their wealth and position to strangle the freedom that was man's natural right, then it was time to form a body of resistance to such a gross perversion of God's laws. He fought for man's right to serve in complete liberty of body, mind and heart, his trade, his master and his Lord.

It is necessary to realize that these three parties who were roused to interest in the Tolpuddle Labourers' Martyrdom had lost the true significance of the ideal behind the action, because they all saw it from but one point of view. The labourers were sacrificed—unwittingly it may be—not for a party, not for a policy, not even for a particular creed, but to proclaim man's freedom of expression in all those respects.

This, then, is the story of the Tolpuddle Martyrs, and it is a great little bit of history which can never be forgotten by students of social conditions in nineteenth-century England, or by those interested in the growth of trade unionism. The story is only one stone in that great structure which we call English History. It is neither a foundation nor a key-stone, but nevertheless without such stones the building would be incomplete, and it bears just enough of the tracery of individual suffering and heroism to command the admiration of those who recognize beautiful workmanship and who would do honour to the craftsmen who designed and accomplished it.

CHAPTER V

THE CAUSES OF UNREST

THE early years of the nineteenth century were a golden age for farmers. As George Eliot says: 'It was still that glorious war-time which was felt to be a peculiar favour of Providence towards the landed interest, and the fall of prices had not come to carry the race of small squires and yeomen down that road to ruin for which extravagant habits and bad husbandry were plentifully anointing their wheels.' So long as there is no invasion, war means profit for farmers. It was so even from 1914 to 1918. But that war was too short to create a habit of prosperity, or lure the farming class into imagining that the rise in prices was permanent. Besides, there were other factors at work which made the war-time in the early twentieth century different from the war-time of the early nineteenth century, from the farmers' point of view. England had other sources of food supply for the greater part of the four years; and conscription made it difficult for farmers to find the necessary labour, or indeed to be able themselves to enjoy the prosperity of their business. The long years of the Napoleonic wars had no such disadvantages for the farmers and landowners. They could demand a monopoly price for the food produced from the land. They should have been in clover; but were they?

The evidence is contradictory. Big profits are not necessarily a sign of true prosperity. And various circumstances combined to cause violent fluctuations in prices, which are the bane of the industrious and honest producer. By 1834 the agricultural industry generally had had full experience of a drop in prices. Even earlier than that date William Cobbett gives a picture of the farmers' position which does not accord with the account of George Eliot and other writers. Probably he looked deeper into the problem; but at the same time it is necessary to discount a good deal of his outcry, for political prejudice made him exaggerate the dark shades of his picture. In his view the farmer was the victim of rapacious landowners and tithe-owners backed up by an iniquitous Government which taxed the land out of cultivation, to support a host of sycophant placeholders. He attributed falling prices, the misery of the labourers, and every other evil, to the same cause:

> I passed through that villainous hole, Cricklade, about two hours ago; and, certainly, a more rascally looking place I never set my eyes on. I wished to avoid it, but could get along no other way. . . . The labourers seem miserably poor. Their dwellings are little better than pig-beds, and their looks indicate that their food is not nearly equal to that of a pig. Their wretched hovels are stuck upon little bits of ground *on the road-side*, where the space has been wider than the road demanded. In many places they have not two rods to a hovel. It seems as if they had been swept off the fields by a hurricane, and had dropped and found shelter under the banks on the road-side! Yesterday morning was a sharp frost; and this had set the poor creatures to digging up their little plats of potatoes. In my whole life I never saw human wretchedness equal to this: no, not even amongst the free negroes in America, who, on an average, do not work one day out of four. And this is '*prosperity*' is it? These, O Pitt! are the fruits of thy hellish system![1]

Cobbett's political views are not our concern.

[1] *Rural Rides*, Nov. 7, 1831.

But as an observer and reporter he was unequalled. He knew the conditions about which he was writing from practical experience; and he wrote with sympathy, honesty, and utter fearlessness. There could be no more trustworthy witness to the condition of the agricultural labourer in the years 1821-1831, and therefore, to those causes of unrest which precipitated the events of 1834. The facts are plain: whether the fault lay with the farmers, the landowners, or the Government, it was always the bottom-dog who bore the brunt of suffering.

We get another account, written a few years later, of life in Dorset in 1795. A valuable and rare book, published by Mr. David Davies, the rector of Barkham, gives an authentic survey in *The Case of the Labourers in Husbandry*, of the 'probable causes of the distresses of the poor which are the rise of the price of necessaries, the buying them at the dearest hand, the low and unproportionate price of labour, the increasing scarcity of employment for the poor, and their own want of industry, having no encouragement given them. Many working men breakfast and dine on dry bread alone, without cheese or drink of any kind; their meal is supper, and that generally no better than unpeeled potatoes and salt, or barley-cake fried, and water. Clothes they get as they can, and the children go nearly naked. There is little work now for lads, and that at a reduced price; 2d. or 3d. a day, instead of 4d. or 5d., which it was formerly.' He gives a typical budget for a family of six persons for a week's provisions, etc:

	s.	d.
Bread and Flour	6	0
Yeast and Salt		2
Bacon and other meat		8
Tea, Sugar, Butter, Cream		10
Cheese		3
Beer		2
Soap, Starch, Blue		1
Candles		$2\frac{1}{2}$
Thread, etc.		$0\frac{3}{4}$
Potatoes and Barley		2
	8	$7\frac{1}{4}$

Even this meagre expenditure would have had to be cut down thirty years later, as the standard rate of wage for Dorset was then, as has already been stated, but 7s. per week.

The labourers suffered, be it remembered, not merely as animals—hunger, thirst, cold, weariness—but as men. They felt the injustice as well as the discomfort of their condition. They could contrast the present with what they had heard of the past: they could be roused to visions of the future. They thought less of themselves than of their wives and children. They had an ingrained patriotism, inarticulate but somehow blended with love of the land:

So to the land our hearts we give
  Till the sure magic strike,
And Memory, Use and Love make live
  Us and our fields alike—
That deeper than our speech and thought
  Beyond our reasons sway
Clay of the pit whence we were wrought
  Yearns to its fellow-clay.

This point is so important, that the labourers were resentful because they were men, with human instincts, human feelings, human powers of reasoning—that even at the risk of repeating what has already been touched upon, we must emphasize these two factors of love of the land and the sense of injustice, if we are to understand the Tolpuddle tragedy.

Many a Britisher, after a night journey through France, is amazed when he wakes up in the early morning to see whole families of peasants already at work in their fields. He is amazed, because he comes from a country where love of the land has been almost stamped out. Millions of men and women in France are wedded to the soil: in England it is more often the peasant's ambition to get away from the soil to the glamour of town-life. It has not always been so; yeoman means village-man; and for many centuries the yeomen of England were the backbone of the nation, not only in peace but also in war. They were men who had a stake in the country because they possessed some of it, and they loved what they possessed with a deep-rooted passion such as no townsman could feel.

This is not the opportunity for explaining at any length the system of land tenure in England up to the time of the Enclosure Acts. As a matter of fact there were many systems of tenure. What does concern us is this—that the ordinary villager had an important and acknowledged place in the system, a share in the common-field, some rights of pasturage and of fuel-collecting in the waste, perhaps some special plot of private possession. Methods of tillage may have been uneconomic, bad seasons may have led to semi-starvation; but the villager had a stake in the country and an interest in life. It is more than doubtful whether his daily round embraced so many may-poles or his common task enabled him to quaff so many gallons of nut-brown ale as Mr. Belloc or Mr. Chesterton would have us believe. But he was free. And if the land failed to produce all the wheat it was capable of producing, it produced something much better, a sturdy and self-respecting peasantry. The exigencies of war and the growing cult of efficiency changed all that. The apostles of efficiency are more concerned with statistics than with human life. And war is a taskmaster who demands sacrifices even away from the battlefield. War demanded that England should produce more wheat; therefore nothing must be allowed to stand in the way of agricultural efficiency. If the village community and the free labourer were economic anachronisms, they must go. What did tradition matter; what did contentment matter; what did love of the land matter; what did justice matter?

The cry for efficiency was at the root of the Enclosure Acts—let us be fair about this. But it let loose baser motives. The big landowner was glad to become a bigger landowner. He was glad to be able to crush the tiresome independence of the villagers. The needs of the time gave him the advantage of being able to shelter himself behind the cry of patriotism. But the villagers of course knew little or nothing about the glory of war, and economic efficiency, and the intensive culture of wheat. All they knew was what they experienced, the loss of their cherished possessions and privileges. It seemed to them that what the little man lost the big man gained. So the legend has grown up that the Enclosure Acts were simply acts of grab, whereby the strong despoiled the weak. Yet no one can doubt that many who voted in Parliament in favour of enclosure, and many who supported the policy outside, were genuinely convinced that it was a necessary and inevitable measure for saving the country from starvation. The whole matter is summed up with judicial impartiality by Sir Frederick Pollock in his book on the Land Laws:—'Wholesale enclosure, begun in more or less irregular ways in the sixteenth century, was the deliberate policy of the social reformers and philanthropists of the eighteenth. To bring as much land as possible under cultivation seemed to them the just ambition of the landowner who would serve the commonwealth.' What had been going on gradually for centuries was given the note of urgency by the Napoleonic wars, and by the immense increase in population which began about the same time.

The process of despoiling the labourer was so slow that the memory of his rights was never lost. Fathers told their sons of happier days, and could appeal to grandfather to verify tradition. No doubt the golden mist of memory veiled many of the drawbacks of olden times. But so long as men attached any value to freedom, they were driven to look back for the last traces of it. It is true that 'the poor never lost a right without being congratulated by the rich on gaining something better'; but they were pig-headed enough to imagine that they were themselves the best judges of the value of what they had lost. Had they been articulate they might well have asked, 'What shall it profit a man if he shall gain the whole world and lose his own soul?' The resentment which they felt vented itself, in ways which were often foolish, on the immediate causes of the change in their condition; they broke the machines, for instance, which seemed to be throwing them out of work. But this lawlessness made no appeal to the more thoughtful of them, men like George Loveless and his comrades, who resented the sapping of their manhood, and found their rallying-point in the cry for freedom.

It is tempting to quote page after page of the appalling but fascinating records of the administration of the Enclosure Acts, collected by the Hammonds. They expose it as one of the blackest blots on our national history. Hypocrisy, cheating, and cruelty marked every step of the way. Human nature was seen at its foulest; for men treated their fellow-men far worse than they treated their cattle or their pigs. We must content ourselves, however, with one quotation, not of lurid happenings, but of the contrast which must have occupied the ordinary labourer's mind as he compared his present position with the tradition of the past: 'In an unenclosed village the normal labourer did not depend on his wages alone. His livelihood was made up from various sources. His firing he took from the waste, he had a cow or a pig wandering on the common pasture, perhaps he raised a little crop on a strip of the common fields. He was not merely a wage earner, receiving so much money a week or a day for his labour, and buying all the necessaries of life at a shop: he received wages as a labourer, but in part he maintained himself as a producer. Further, the actual money revenue of the family was not limited to the labourer's earnings, for the domestic industries that flourished in the village gave employment to his wife and children.' Gleaning, too, was a much valued privilege, for in some cases it enabled families to gather as much wheat as would keep them in bread for a year, or as many beans as would keep a pig. 'In an enclosed village . . . the position of the agricultural labourer was very different. All his auxiliary resources had been taken from him, and he was now a wage earner and nothing more. Enclosure had robbed him of the strip that he tilled, of the cow that he kept on the village pasture, of the fuel that he picked up in the woods, and of the turf he tore from the common. And while a social revolution had swept away his possessions, an industrial revolution had swept away his family's earnings. To families living on the scale of the village poor, each of these losses was a crippling blow, and the total effect of the changes was to destroy their economic independence.'[1] It is worth noting that the value of the subsidiary means of livelihood must have varied from village to village. In some there was little pasture, in others no woods, in others no turf to be cut. But anyone who knows Tolpuddle will realize how rich the parish must have been in all these respects.

We cannot undertake a survey of the unrest which seethed among the agricultural labourers of England about 1830. But it will help to explain

[1] Hammond, J. L. and B. *The Village Labourer*, Chap. V.

the particular incident with which we are concerned if we say something about what was happening in Dorset at this time. Rioting was much less serious than it had been in Hampshire and Wiltshire. There was little violence beyond the breaking up of some of the obnoxious threshing-machines, and the firing of some ricks. Even when the starving mob demanded money, they only used threats. And in the case of one man, George Legg, on whom sentence of death was pronounced, the worst that could be said was that he 'talked rough and bobbish', when he and some of his fellow-labourers demanded 1s. 6d. from Farmer Morey. This iniquitous sentence (which was not carried out) was pronounced at Dorchester, where a Special Commission, appointed to try rioters, opened on January 11th, 1831. Their labours were so meagre in comparison with what had taken place elsewhere that *The Times* complained that the pomp and expense of a Special Commission were not justified.

Dorset may have been quieter than the neighbouring counties, but it does not follow that the fears of the landowners were less. Private letters, often the most trustworthy evidence of atmosphere, reveal a state of mind bordering on panic. Mr. E. Berkeley Portman writes to his friend,

Mr. Okeden, from Bryanston, on November 27th, 1830:

> We are all safe in our division, and have organized our matters so well that we can assemble 200 armed and mounted and about 2,000 pedestrian special constables ready to resist any mob. If you want the aid of our horsemen send to me or to Mr. Farquharson and we will be with you in a trice, but do not send without full and certain cause. The chief danger now, is from talk and reports which are untrue and exaggerated. When all is quiet we will meet and talk about wages of labour, and we must have a special general sessions to try the machine breaking committed. A troop of Lancers is just come to Blandford, and we shall send them on to Dorchester unless we hear that you want them by any special messenger to-night, as they *ought* to be at Dorchester.

It seems strange that an irregular army of 200 horse and 2,000 foot, backed up by a troop of regular Cavalry, should be thought necessary to deal with the 'mobs' of a sparsely populated agricultural neighbourhood, in which the chief disorders were due to small bodies of half-starved men acting by night. In fact a good deal of the damage which so terrified the landowners was done, apparently, by lone adventurers. At any rate, this may be inferred from an official Printed Notice issued from Blandford:

> It is strongly suspected that most of the FIRES have been caused by TWO MEN, who have been seen near the spot either a short time before, or immediately after their breaking out. They have been making enquiries of Shepherds, and Labourers respecting the Situations of Farms, and different Circumstances relating to them. One is about 40 years of age, rides a light-carcassed, sorrel-coloured horse, what is vulgarly called a Blood-Horse, with a Switch Tail; wears Knee-caps or Over-alls, sometimes has a Drab Great Coat; generally is seen riding fast through Villages or Towns, with something different from a common riding Stick, with which he is constantly striking the Horse's Off-Shoulder. The other rides a Black Horse of the same long-legged Description; they are dressed and look like Farmers. It is supposed that the thing which is carried in the hand is an Air Gun, from which a small Shell is thrown, which ignites after a certain time. It is supposed that in Dorset the Incendiaries are travelling on foot in different disguises making the same enquiries as above.

If an Official Document could describe so remarkable a figure as this man in Knee-caps, riding what is vulgarly called a Blood-Horse, and constantly striking its Off-Shoulder with an Air Gun from which a small Shell is thrown, imagination reels at what Rumour might describe. It was, however, mysterious individuals of this description who were the terror of the countryside, rather than the little bands of angry yokels who knew they had to face overwhelming numbers of armed special constables or even a troop of regular cavalry. The chief of all these mystery-men was known as 'Captain Swing'. He remained anonymous, and he was never identified or caught. But the exploits attributed to him were legion, and the panic he caused spread not just in one neighbourhood, but through the length and breadth of the country. Mr. Castleman of Wimborne received a typical 'Swing' letter in this panicky year, 1830:

> Sir,—Sunday night your House shall come down to the Ground for you are an inhuman monster and we will dash out your brains—Banks and your sett aught to be sent to Hell. The Hanley Torches have not forgot you.

There is no record, in this case, that Swing's bite proved equal to his bark, or that Castleman, Banks, and their fellow squires suffered the fate suggested for them. But every threat and every rumour added fuel to the fire of fear.

Moreton House, the home of Squire Frampton, was put in a state of defence as if to withstand a siege. And yet nothing had happened and nothing did happen to justify such measures. It is clear from Mary Frampton's diary that, to put it plainly, the squires had lost their nerve. Her entry for November 28th, 1830, records:

> Many threats had been reported to us as having been made in the course of the day, and during the dispersion of the mob against Mr. Frampton's person and property, but no fire took place on his estate. There was one announced to us watchers, but not being very near Moreton we had nothing to do but to lament over the wickedness which occasioned that and so many other incendiary fires. There were no soldiers in the county, all having been sent towards London, Wiltshire, and Hampshire, where the riots raged first, and in the beginning of December hourly accounts of the assembling of mobs for the purpose of breaking the thrashing machines, increase of wages, and extorting money, etc., arrived. Under these circumstances it was judged necessary to block up all the lower windows of Moreton House, as well as all the doors, with the exception of that to the offices. The Mayor of Dorchester ordered the staff of Dorset Militia to go to Moreton to defend the house, nightly patrols were established and

> Mr. Frampton or his son sat up alternately for many nights. My sister-in-law also took her turn in sitting up with another woman, Lady Frampton saying that they were more watchful than men. Spies were certainly sent from the rioters to see the state of the house, etc.

It may be well to explain that the 'riot' which led to all these precautions occurred at Winfrith. There was no violence. Mr. Frampton, *accompanied by 150 special-constables*, appeared on the scene. 'The mob . . . advanced rather respectfully and with their hats in their hands, to demand increases of wages, but would not listen to the request that they should disperse. . . . The whole body of the police then advanced with Mr. Frampton, and after an ineffectual parley, charged them, when three men were taken and were conveyed by my brother and his son, Henry, to Dorchester and committed to gaol.' Though Mr. Portman had written on November 27th that a troop of Lancers was at Blandford and would be transferred to Dorchester, Miss Frampton apparently knew nothing about it. This was perhaps due to the fact that relations were strained between the Framptons and Mr. Portman who had 'promised to raise the wages of his labourers, and by doing this without concert with other gentlemen greatly increased their difficulties'. It is worthy to note that Moreton is only five or six miles from Tolpuddle, and that Mr. Frampton, who barricaded his house in terror in 1830, was in a position to show himself harsh and vindictive, without danger, in 1834.

This general survey of the position in Dorset in the years immediately preceding the Tolpuddle Tragedy helps to explain how some such event was almost inevitable. The squires, after a time of panic, had conquered through the efforts of the Government and the Special Commission which sat at Dorchester in January, 1831, to deal with the rioters. They were not men to forget or forgive. So when Freedom began to raise her head again, they lost all sense of justice and harried the Martyrs by persecution and false witness. The reaction from fear made bullies of them. How abnormal were the feelings of the time may be learned from another entry in the diary of Mary Frampton, whose prejudices seem to have come into conflict with her natural kindness of heart, and led her into an illuminating and very suggestive state of self-contradiction. After the Special Commission of 1831, she writes: 'Parliament opened on Feb. 3rd. There was a petition to the King to pardon all the unhappy men who had been convicted at special assizes. Fortunately, however, as they were already on board the transports and the wind fair, the petition would be too late. Care was taken at the deportation of these men to keep them separate from convicts of a different description and to send them to those parts of New Zealand and New Holland where their agricultural knowledge and labour might be useful. Thus very probably at a future time rendering our disturbances here a blessing to our Antipodies.'

This conclusion requires no comment; its sublime ignoring of all humanity in the sufferers throws a flood of light on the causes of their suffering, and on subsequent sufferings in 1834.

CHAPTER VI

THE FRUITS OF DEFEAT

NATIONS are saved by the 'seven thousand who have not bowed the knee to Baal'. It is the few who save the many. By sacrifice, and often by defeat, advance is made. The democratic principle that there is something sacred about a majority vote is constantly breaking down in the working, although its utility in many respects is unquestioned. But utility is not the final standard of values in human affairs. There was little of utility in the crazy fight of Sir Richard Grenville in the little *Revenge* against overwhelming odds or in the Charge of the Light Brigade. Yet it is an undoubted fact that such incidents have done more to maintain a worthy national spirit than the plans of utilitarian politicians or the decisive vote of a democratic majority. There is nothing fanciful in believing that the epic story of Scott's Last Voyage to the Antarctic, the greatest heroic drama of modern times, did something towards keeping awake the spirit of gallant adventure in an age which, superficially, was acquisitive and luxury-loving.

The Martyrs of Tolpuddle could neither know nor foresee the reward of their devotion. It was on a higher plane than the plane of utility. Their martyrdom had neither the object nor the result of causing successful trade unions to spring up like mushrooms in the Dorset countryside. It was set in an atmosphere of trade unionism, but its implications were on a wider scale. So there is no reason to be disappointed at the comparative failure of the trade union movement among agricultural labourers, or to think that the heroism of these six pioneers was wasted. There are ways of achieving freedom and fair wages even apart from the official programme of the T.U.C. Indeed, it is doubtful how far methods of safeguarding the well-being of the workers—methods which necessarily have matured in factories, workshops, shipping-yards, and mines—can be adapted to the problems of so variegated an industry as agriculture.

The success of trade unionism among agricultural labourers was but fleeting, and to a large extent it centred on the personality of one man. Moreover, that man came to see, before he died, that there may be 'ways of achieving freedom and fair wages' for the agricultural labourer, apart from that offshoot of the trade union movement which he himself had fostered. Joseph Arch, the greatest of all leaders in agricultural trade unionism, was gradually converted to the belief that it was in Parliament that most could be done for the betterment of the workers in an industry where combined action was extraordinarily difficult, if not impossible.

The record of his National Agricultural Labourers Union is an interesting footnote to the story we are telling of Tolpuddle, and a necessary reminder that you cannot always achieve the same object by employing the same methods. The wiser leaders of trade unionism will not exploit the Centenary for an advertisement of their movement as a panacea for all ills. The problem of bettering the lot of the worker is a human problem; it cannot be solved by some political formula, but only by a sensible adaptability in the use of methods to meet varying needs. It was the realization of this truth that, above everything else, bore witness to Joseph Arch's greatness. His story reads like a continuation of the story of George Loveless. He, too, was a lay-preacher of the Methodist Connexion. Born in 1826, a labourer on the land, a Methodist, a lover of liberty, he must have been inspired by the martyrdom of his older contemporary. No doubt he owed to it an immunity from the cruder forms of persecution; the authorities had learned that freedom cannot be stifled by force. Yet, in spite of some success, this second wave of trade unionism among agricultural labourers was, in effect, fighting a losing battle, and met with the same bitter opposition as the first:

> In many villages the mere formation of a branch led to an instantaneous rise of wages. But, as in 1833-4, the audacity of the field labourer in imitating the combination of the town artisan, provoked an almost indescribable bitterness of feeling on the part of the squirarchy and their connections. The farmers, wherever they dared, 'victimized' any man who joined the Union. It is needless to say that they received the cordial support of the rural magistracy. In aid of a lock-out near Chipping Norton, two justices, who happened both to be clergymen, sent sixteen labourers' wives, some with infants at the breast, to prison with hard labour, for 'intimidating' certain non-Union men. . . . Innumerable acts of petty tyranny and oppression proved how far the landed interest had lagged behind the capitalist employers in the matter of Freedom of Combination. Nor was the Established Church more

> sympathetic. . . . And the farmers, the squires, and the Church were supported by the army. When the labourers in August, 1872, struck for an increase of wages, the officers, in Oxfordshire and Berkshire, placed the soldiers at the disposal of the farmers for the purpose of getting in the harvest and so defeating the Union.

It is obvious, too, that though a strike in the summer might inconvenience the farmers and achieve some measure of success in enforcing a claim for increased wages, the success could only be temporary. For when winter came, and work was slack, the farmers could reply with a lock-out which had devastating consequences for the labourers at a time when food and fuel were scarce. These points are only too clearly exemplified in the record of Joseph Arch's crusade.

In his native Warwickshire he founded a small union, but so compelling was his influence that in 1872 the local union expanded into the National Agricultural Labourers Union, and many who joined it imagined that an industrial millennium was at hand. In two years the membership of the Union grew to 86,000. But 1874 was its zenith; in 1889 the membership had dropped to 5,000, and after various fluctuations the N.A.L.U. expired about 1902. Perhaps it had done its work: at any rate it had given its founder a position and an authority in the House of Commons which, in his opinion, enabled him to do more for his mates than by continuing the superhuman task of holding together workers in an industry so heterogeneous as agriculture.

There can be little doubt that he was right. He was a man great enough to be converted by the force of facts. Ardent trade unionist though he was at first, he changed his tactics when it became clear to him that collective bargaining could never be a success in the agricultural industry, and that the rights of the workers must be safeguarded by the State. This does not mean that his earlier efforts were futile. On the contrary, they were well worth while, for they roused the workers to a greater self-respect, and they helped to make the nation realize the paramount importance of agriculture, and the miserable condition of the agricultural labourer. Joseph Arch's campaign was not in the end a triumph for trade unionism; it was a triumph for reform; just as the Tolpuddle martyrdom was not a triumph for trade unionism but a triumph for reform. The betterment of conditions in industry may be brought about in many ways, and the men who do most for it are not those who try to apply some political panacea and shut their eyes to other methods. It is the men of vision, who fight and suffer for the rights of men as men, who win the biggest battles for mankind. At the risk of repetition we want to make it perfectly clear that the whole nation, and not just one political group, must join in the Centenary tribute to these six apostles of Freedom.

The fruits of their sacrifice have still to be reaped. We hope it may be the task of this generation to reap them. The harvest has been long deferred; and certainly the men who sowed the seed never even began the reaping. The cause for which they strove made little progress after their return from exile. As we have seen, trade unionism did little for the labourer. There seemed more prospect of improvement through legislation, but the prospect has become somewhat of a will-o'-the-wisp and keeps receding. Nevertheless, real progress has been made in the education of public opinion, even while the improvement in actual conditions has been desperately disappointing. Twelve years after the transportation of the Tolpuddle men, the condition of the Dorset labourers was little better than in 1834. But consciences were awakening. We have the witness and example of an enlightened and sympathetic squire on these two points. Richard Brinsley Sheridan, grandson of the playwright and statesman, married the heiress of Frampton Court, Dorset, and came into the property. He was a man of wider vision than most of the neighbouring landowners. He was also a Member of Parliament, and a student of public affairs. Most important of all, he took care to get his information first-hand. In a letter to *The Times* dated May 3rd, 1846, he writes:

> Although much good has been effected in the county of Dorset, by the disclosures which have appeared from time to time in the public prints with reference to the abject condition of the agricultural poor in that county, still the practice (it might almost be called an agreement) continues amongst employers generally of keeping the unfortunate laborer at the rate of wages shamefully disproportionate to his services, and barely sufficient in many instances, to save him from starvation.—My visit to the dwellings of these poor people chanced to be at their dinner hour, when I found that the meal they were about to partake of consisted merely of a small quantity of horse-beans and turnip-tops, boiled in water. I asked the wife of one of the men what she intended to prepare for her husband's supper when he returned home from his hard day's work, and her answer was, in the most cheerful tone, 'Why, bless you, Sir, horse-beans and turnip-tops.' I believe this to be the

condition of the agricultural laborers generally in the West part of the county of Dorset—I know it to be so in the parish of Bettiscombe and the adjoining parishes.—It matters not, I am convinced, what the rent of a farm may be, or whether a lease is granted or not; whether the price of wheat may be £20 or £10 per load; whether the demand for labor is abundant or not, the average amount of wages in the county of Dorset remains always the same at 7s. per week.

Such was the witness of a sympathetic observer. But he also enclosed a letter which he had received from some of the men themselves. It reveals, in its simple pathos, an attitude of mind which claimed and claims careful consideration by those who have the good of the labourer at heart:

Sir, your Honour—We, poor laborers, make bold to lay our case before you: we hope and trust no offence. We beg to state that we laborers are great sufferers, our wages being so low, our living so scanty, we have not sufficient to keep our strength to work. When we complain they say that the Gentlemen will not put their little fingers to help them, which we know to be wrong, because we know that all repairs are paid, although they try to blind us. Let not your Honour be angry with our statement; our trials are great and insupportable; the farmers' behaviour to poor laborers cannot be pleasing in the sight of God. Is it not said in Holy Writ, 'Muzzle not the mouth of the ox, for the laborer is worthy of his hire'? We work hard for a little money; our wages is 1s. 2d. per day. What is that with a small family not able to do anything? Out of which we have to pay 1s. 6d. per week house-rent; then there is soap, candles, bed-linen, clothing, shoes, and working tools all to be taken out of our little earnings; then what have we left for food?—We leave your Honour to judge; and to add to our trials, the potato crops failed; we feel the want of them—We wish the farmers were not so hard with us. We believe a great part of it is hid from your eyes. We believe your Honour to be a friend to the poor. The Lord knoweth the oppressor and the oppressed; there is nothing hid from His all-seeing eye. We poor laborers are oppressed, and on the failure of the potato crops it has made our distress the greater. The farmers' behaviour to us are, that when we do any job-work we generally do it before we know what we are going to have for it, and then they will give us what they like—they will not let us earn more than 7s. a week if they can help it, which makes our lives bitter and rather wish for the grave—We beg your pardon for not inserting our names, for if our employers know what we have written they would despise us, and we should be discharged. —The Poor Humble and Obedient Labourers.

Their trust in Mr. Sheridan was not misplaced. He did what he could. But the farmers were, for the most part, stubborn and vindictive, so that he would only have made the condition of the labourers worse by taking up their case too vigorously. The best he could do was to stir up public opinion. And public opinion shows a strange unreadiness to respond to the rather inarticulate appeal of the poor worker on the land.

Even in 1868, when the price of produce was high and Dorset was at the zenith of agricultural prosperity, the condition of the labourers was not much better than it had been in 1834 or in 1846. Cottages were often hovels. The water supply was often unwholesome and inadequate, and drainage non-existent. The custom existed in most parts of the county of hiring whole families, and making the women and children work for a miserable additional pittance. No doubt there was some gradual improvement, but it was so gradual that it is difficult to trace. Up to 1914 the ordinary agricultural labourer in Dorset would get, for wages, about 12s. a week in money, and the rest in 'allowances'—worth perhaps 3s. It was not a living wage, and contrasted unfavourably with the rising wages and improved standard of living which marked the condition of the workers in towns. The British public were still ignorant of two vital facts—that the work of labourers on the land is a highly skilled job, and that agriculture is the basic industry of every prosperous nation.

It is outside the scope of this book to attempt any detailed account of how the position of the agricultural labourer has improved in the last hundred years. The fruits of 1834 have taken a long time to mature. But anyone who has studied the history of the time must know that it is by legislation, and by a more sympathetic public opinion, that some change for the better has been brought about. There is still much to be done; a truer independence and a greater fixity of tenure to be won for the labourer. Perhaps, more particularly—though the ordinary townsman does not understand its importance—an effort should be made to satisfy the land-hunger which possesses the best type of land-worker. Every man who works on the land for another man should have a bit of land of his own, not as a concession but as a right. This would give stability to what must be, at best, an unstable form of industry. For hours and conditions of labour cannot be settled by rule as they can in a factory. There must be times of stress and times of comparative stagnation in agriculture. A period of hard frost can scarcely be as busy as when the hay-crop has to be got in with the prospect of rain ahead. But if some reasonable limits are set to hours of labour—by means of wage-boards or in some other way—if a living wage is assured, and a man has a cottage and a piece of land where he can grow vegetables and perhaps keep a pig—then, England may have a contented and settled body of peasantry such as has always proved the backbone of every great commonwealth.

CHAPTER VII

THEN AND NOW

IN the history of the Tolpuddle Martyrs we have tried to deal impartially with the subject, and not magnify unduly either the event itself or the consequences which accrued. We have tried to fit it into an appropriate setting of time and place, so that readers may realize the vast differences that existed in the conditions of living in those days, and made this incident, not only possible, but to some extent, excusable. The calculable results are definitely hard to assess; the most that can truly be claimed is that it served as a signpost. A signpost does not proceed anywhere itself, but it indicates to a wayfarer the best road to a given destination down which he may travel. The Tolpuddle signpost pointed out the way to 'Improved Conditions for Agricultural Labourers' and 'A Greater Liberty'. And the highway to be traversed was the way of 'Public Opinion'. It is thus that nearly all reforms have been wrought in England, not in an apathetic acquiescence in imperfect conditions, nor by red revolution, but by the slow education of a public conscience. The Tolpuddle event showed itself to be peculiarly British in this respect. In many another country, the public protest might have terminated either in active revolt, with the breaking of heads and the spilling of blood, or, after a brief period of excited expostulation, the victims would have been forgotten and left to work out the full term of their sentence. Not so in England, however; the public conscience, roused by the stubborn persistence of a few, saw to it that justice should right the wrong that had been committed, and that reparation should be made.

Public opinion, in this instance, had only been awakened to a whirlwind activity in a specific case, and it now died down to a murmuring breeze, stirring amongst the malcontents in field and farm-yard, and the idlers round the village pump. It had yet to be converted to the urgency of the full task that lay before it—that of securing for agricultural labour sufficient means to maintain a decent standard of life. This should be a right to which every self-respecting worker should consider himself entitled, and should be the first charge on a country that values its people.

Cobbett affirmed that he wrote much 'the object of which was to induce the labourers resolutely to maintain the rights which, agreeably to the laws of our country, we had all inherited from our forefathers. Amongst these rights was the right to live in the country of our birth; the right to have a living out of the land of our birth in exchange for our labour duly and honestly performed; the right, in case we fell into distress, to have our wants sufficiently relieved out of the produce of the land, whether that distress arose from sickness, from decrepitude, from old age, or from inability to find employment.' We reiterate that it was many years before reform was accomplished, but could Cobbett return now, he might consider that his Utopian vision had more or less materialized. There is none born in this country, who does not feel that he has the right to remain in it. Emigration, even for the sake of relieving an over-populated land, has never been forced on its people. Not yet have we taken to redistributing the population by the arbitrary transportation of one million townsfolk to country areas as in Soviet Russia! Needless to say, the scarcity of employment has compelled many to earn their living in other lands, but banishment from their own country is an obligation laid on no one.

Would Cobbett consider that the farm-labourers of to-day receive a wage sufficient to reward them for 'their labour duly and honestly performed'? It is hard to estimate, for the standard of living maintained by wage-earners of to-day is in many respects little short of what their forebears would have considered luxurious. We hear of great poverty in certain areas, notably on the East Coast: there may be much inward privation that belies the outward visible sign of comfort and prosperity which pervades so many cottage homes. Many gardens there are that display the hop-pole (in various attitudes of intoxicated obliquity), which does duty for a wireless aerial and through its agency, dance-bands and 'variety programmes' are enabled to violate the peace of countryside. Visit the village schools and note the warm and sensible clothing of the lads and lasses: their bodies are well-nourished, their feet well-shod. Certainly, to the superficial observer, there seems little actual need in rural England. Mention might be made of the immense sums that are being deposited week by week in the National Savings—sometimes totalling a million pounds a week. A by no means negligible part of this is contributed from the villages, through the schools, Women's Institutes, etc. It is a splendid movement, because it provides the labouring classes once again with a stake in their country, which they lost when land was taken from them as a result of the Enclosure Acts. Landlords maintain their cottage property in a better state of repair than in former years; more villages than ever before have an adequate drainage system, and many of them are supplied with a main water supply.

Cobbett bade the labourers expect to have 'their wants sufficiently relieved out of the produce of the land, whether that distress arose from sickness, from decrepitude, from old age, or from inability to find employment'. Most villages now can depend on the services of a parish nurse, and many districts are joined up with hospital contributory schemes, whereby for a trifling sum a week, a family becomes entitled to free treatment at the local hospital. The Health Insurance benefit keeps a family going whilst the bread-winner is laid up, and the Old Age Pension is a great boon, adding a stimulus to saving sufficient during the working days to supplement the pension and thus ensure an old age fairly free from financial anxiety. This is a very superficial survey of the progress in recent years of the conditions of living in agricultural areas, but it does tend to show that the seed sown by the Martyrs and their contemporaries has ripened and borne fruit at long last.

We said that the Tolpuddle signpost indicated the way to 'A Greater Liberty'. How far have we travelled since 1834 in this respect? Here again, the intervening years, have shown extraordinarily slow growth. We remarked in a previous chapter that the demand for efficiency has resulted in a loss of individualism in trade, agriculture and industry generally. We see it on every side in the craze for Big Business. Individual enterprise is being squeezed out to make room for capitalized combines, which are mopping up smaller tradesfolk, who have no chance to compete against the cut prices and other advantages possible to business on such a wholesale basis. Combines, partnerships, amalgamations of all kinds are the order of the day. There is another factor in social life which seems to militate against the freedom of the individual in these days, and that is the increase of governmental—both national and local—restrictions on the liberty of the individual. We often hear the cry of the exasperated citizen, that he cannot call his soul his own. As a matter of fact, that is just what he may do, but he may not necessarily call his possessions or his actions his own.

But he must remember that laws are made to protect the right-acting, right-thinking section of the many against the heedlessness and lawlessness of the few.

It seems at first sight a strange anomaly that corporate freedom should in these ways be apparently restricted at a time when greater liberty for the individual is being acknowledged. Before the last of the Martyrs had returned to England, Queen Victoria had ascended the throne and an amazing epoch had been established. Reforms were needed, for Court and upper-class social life, from which middle-class England took its cue, was extravagant, profligate, and unheeding of the responsibilities of its wealth and position. Queen Victoria and her good consort set to work to spring-clean, and in so doing inaugurated a period of puritanism unequalled in national history. The benefit that the country derived in the long run cannot be sufficiently estimated, but it had its evil consequences; the nation was rescued from galloping down-hill to the dogs, but it was driven into a prison-house of conventionality and conservatism which was stultifying in its effect.

With the advent of this century, and still more since the Great War, we see the breakdown of much of this conventionality and traditionalism, and an increase in the liberty of the individual. Conduct is governed nowadays, not by deference to custom or tradition, but by individual conscience. Work and play are not the prerogative of any particular class, but both are rights to which all men and women consider themselves entitled. Individual opinion is expressed freely in politics, religion, art, etc., and no one is condemned or taboo because of the extraordinary views that he holds. Class distinctions are disappearing; the modern child is mixed up from his earliest years in education with children in all grades of society. 'Die-hard' representatives of the old aristocracy may deplore the mixture to be found in the most select of public schools, but educationalists approve of the resulting interchange of ideas and ideals which tend to eliminate class prejudices and complexes. The annual camp for public school boys and working lads inaugurated by the Duke of York is an admirable embodiment of the new spirit.

We believe that alongside this new freedom is growing up an increased individual and class self-respect. A fatherly Government fosters this spirit. A mother is apt to think far more of her Tommy since the State finds it necessary to insist on the removal of his tonsils, or of her Maggie, because authority decrees that her unbecoming squint should be rectified. The care and attention that the children receive in their school life has its reflection in the home conditions, and more British cottage-homes are models of cleanliness and comfort than at any previous period.

This point—the growth of self-respect in individuals—is not unimportant; it may be that it is by this means that the nation is working out its salvation, and that through the development of a self-respecting people, a social conscience will emerge, that can be relied on to safeguard the interests of the community. Indeed it may be here that we may find a partial explanation of the failure of democracy in other countries. After the War, revolt against authority and a passionate desire for individual freedom, were not confined to this country alone, and there was a universal spirit of restlessness and dissatisfaction abroad. Governments became panicky; they feared a breakdown in civilization—a French Revolution on a large scale, where freedom unbacked by principle developed into licence. Communism, Fascism, Nazi-ism, all in their own way, express their national reaction to this fear. Such a reaction against our constituted government is unlikely in England; we are too independent a people to be attracted by methods of dictatorship. It is for this reason that some say that the day of the trade unions is over. They did their work at a time when the flood of the Industrial Revolution had overborne the good judgment and benevolence of the employing classes, who had sacrificed to their get-rich-quick methods, the voiceless, undefended workers. For the future, the social conscience will safeguard the interests of labour. In combination, the trade unions found their strength; let them beware lest, by carrying on the method too long, the links of co-operation become the shackles binding the workers to a system that is out-worn and out of date. George Loveless might have argued thus. He only 'combined', *faute de mieux*, because no social conscience was awake to the cry of the suffering labourers. He was a dreamer, and his dreams found expression in two verses which he wrote when imprisoned in Dorchester Gaol. They are of no literary value, but maybe they contain a prophecy of the manner in which England would struggle out of the dark night of materialism into the light of a worthier idealism, and the medium through which this nation would ultimately find its soul:

God is our guide from field, from wave,
From plough, the anvil, and the loom,

We come, our country's rights to save,
And speak the tyrant factions' doom,
We raise the watchword 'Liberty';
We will, we will, we will be free.

God is our guide—no swords we draw,
We kindle not war's battle fires,
By reason, union, justice, law,
We claim the birth-right of our sires,
We raise the watchword 'Liberty';
We will, we will, we will be free.

We thus look backwards down the years of the last century and estimate in retrospect, with a surer accuracy, the value of the war waged by the Tolpuddle Martyrs and their contemporaries. The battle was not fought in vain. The country has awoken more and more to the fact that the agricultural labourer is a worthy subject for national care and gratitude and his lot must be safeguarded as far as economic considerations will allow. In 1795 Mr. David Davies wrote the following introduction to his book, to which reference has already been made.

In every nation the welfare and contentment of the lower denominations of people are objects of great importance, and deserving continual attention. For the bulk of every nation consists of such as must earn their daily bread by daily labour. It is to the patient industry of these that the higher ranks are everywhere indebted for most of their enjoyments. It is chiefly on these that every nation depends for its population, strength, and security. All reasonable persons will therefore acknowledge the equity of ensuring to them at least the necessary means of subsistence. But of all the denominations of people in a state, the labourers in husbandry are by far the most valuable. For these are the men, who, being constantly employed in the cultivation of the earth, provide the staff of life for the whole nation. And it is the wives of these men, who rear these hardy broods of children, which, besides supplying the country with the hands it would want, fill up the voids which death is continually making in camps and cities. And since they have thus a peculiar title to public regard, one might expect to see them everywhere comfortably accommodated. Yet even in this kingdom, distinguished as it is for humanity and political wisdom, they have been for some time past suffering peculiar hardships.

His words are as worthy of note by the statesmen and landowners of to-day, as they were by the Board of Agriculture to whom they were addressed one hundred and twenty-eight years ago. Legislation has not always been kind to the countryman, but from the Repeal of the Corn Laws onwards has frequently favoured the town-dweller at the expense of his fellow-worker on the land. The present Government, we believe, is well aware of its responsibilities to agriculture. Landowners, who have brought much of the present distress on themselves and from whom therefore, we are inclined to withhold our sympathy, have at last found the problems of landowning too complicated to be ignored or submitted to the policy of *laissez-faire*, which has been the tragedy of the past. The Great War they could not prevent, nor could they elude its effects. War is a vampire which takes its toll of the resources of a country as well as sucking out the life-blood of its people. The taxes and duties that have been levied to meet war debts and reparations have crippled agriculture as much as any other industry, and closed markets, foreign competition, and high prices of raw materials are among the factors that have made reconstruction difficult. The fall in the price of land, brought about by bad times, is not the least of the troubles with which landowners have had to contend. Facts like the following, given by Sir W. Beach Thomas,[1] cannot be ignored: 'Much of the high land above Marlborough was sold early in this century at £4 an acre freehold. Land not very

[1] *Christianity and the Crisis*

much better is *rented* in Scandinavia for the same price. In Huntingdonshire, a property of 2,000 acres was valued two generations ago at £36,000. It could be bought to-day for £5,000—that is for a sum much below the value of the houses on it.'

The past has told its tale: the pages of the present lie open before us: the future is even now being conceived in the minds of those who are responsible for the reconstruction of the nation, and we believe that, more and more, will the fact be accepted that agriculture is at the root of national prosperity. The 'Back to the Land' slogan was not invented by theorists or impractical visionaries, and the best efforts of every lover of his country must be given towards solving the problems connected therewith.

But the remedy cannot only be found at Westminster; landowners and workers may not wait with folded hands for the return of better times. They must be willing to learn lessons from their continental and colonial neighbours: to be more enterprising in trying new methods of cultivation: to aim at a higher quality of production and to organize a more comprehensive system of distribution. But no amount of enterprise, legislation or increased industrial prosperity will of themselves be sufficient to woo and win success, without the willing co-operation and sacrifice on the part of farmers and landowners and workers. Probably in the future no fortunes will be made on the land, and property owners will have to be satisfied with a comparatively small return on their capital; but a living *will* be made: labourers *will* receive an adequate wage: and a national industry *will* be once more self-supporting.

An authority whom we have consulted considers that the hope of the future lies in parcelling out land in plots of 40 acres or so, where two men—brothers, maybe, or father and son—could do the work between them and run twelve head of cattle, keep pigs, poultry, etc., and make a decent living. If this were done over a large area, the problem of accessible markets might be solved by the construction of regional factories where all the produce could be disposed of. A sufficient living could be made, our authority contends, by some such method, but the work would be hard—and hard work as our colonial brothers know it, seems to have lost its attraction for many of us. We know of a certain parish in Surrey where, after the War, the County Council provided small holdings for ex-service men. Almost without exception the men failed to wring a living out of their holdings. Most of them gave up the attempt within two years. But one of them succeeded and gradually he acquired several of the other holdings and now has a flourishing and extensive dairy business. He was a Dane (who had served in the British Forces) with a wife and five sons. The whole family worked early and late, as none of the other Englishmen similarly circumstanced did, and by sheer concentration of purpose they won through. Determination, a certain amount of business capacity, enterprise—all these qualities are needed by those who live by the cultivation of the land, and the greatest of these is determination.

The country is learning its lesson. Mr. Stanley Baldwin felt himself justified in declaring in 1933 that 'the old idea in the towns that all agricultural troubles were due to the inefficiency of those who work on the land, is exploded once and for all'. And there are other reassuring signs of improvement in the agricultural outlook. In 1933, the Ministry of Agriculture was able to report that there are large increases in the wheat and sugar-beet acreages under cultivation, and that for the first time for ten years the total number of agricultural workers in England and Wales showed an increase. It is encouraging to find that, in Dorset, at any rate, there is greater permanence of service; that whereas labourers were constantly moving from farm to farm, now they remain in the same employment year after year. Furthermore, even the labourers get a minimum wage of 30s. a week, and as methods of farming improve, the percentage of skilled men employed at higher wages grows bigger. The land-worker sees a career opening before him.

Every encouragement as to social conditions should be offered to those who work on the land, and for this purpose the interest and attraction of village life should be increased. Much improvement has taken place in the last few years. There are few villages that are out of reach of some line of country buses, whereby conveyance into the nearest country town can be obtained, and there gaily-dressed shop-windows, Woolworths and cinemas provide interest and amusement for all tastes.

The value of Women's Institutes cannot be overestimated. They are continually creating fresh interest in the lives of the women, are bringing all classes together, and are educating them to realize that homes are not just four walls with a roof overhead, but the meeting-place of a variety of influences, not the least of which are intelligence, domestic efficiency and cultivation of the beautiful. Moreover, they are proving an economic asset in the lives of many cottagers through the establishment in country towns of Women's Institute market stalls, where members from the surrounding districts may send in their surplus garden produce and handcrafts to be retailed to willing purchasers in the towns. The Institutes take turns in providing a selection of their members to sell at the stall, which proves a happy meeting-place for the interchange of ideas, cooking receipts and friendly gossip.

The Rural Community Councils are striving hard to inculcate a 'community' spirit in the mind of the country-dweller, and to break down social barricades and village prejudices which exist even in these sophisticated days, and to foster, by lectures and so forth, a more instructed interest in rural and national problems. Few villages are without clubs of some description, and a recent development is a Federation of Young Farmers' Clubs, which aims at providing their members with technical instruction in stock-farming and horticulture at the same time as encouraging the Club spirit.

But it is not enough merely to interest the older generation in their rural surroundings. There is always a steady drift of young people from the country into the towns, a fact which is to be deplored. Because they have been taught no better, they hopefully imagine that where humanity most congregates, where competition is keenest, where prosperity is expressed in terms of money—there is the milieu where they can best find opportunities of self-expression. 'Because they have been taught no better' was said advisedly. How many children are taught that to delight in simple things is to lay up an inexhaustible and enduring reserve of happiness for life, or are brought to find in the prodigality of Nature's bounty treasures withheld from kings, wealth denied to millionaires; or to find in the tangible and visible creation around them the expression of the eternal God Himself? Nay, often the natural power of appreciation in children remains unsuspected and dies stillborn, through lack of comprehension and vision in their elders. Thomas Traherne wrote in an age far less superficial and material-minded than ours:—'The first Light (the perception of God in the Universe) which shined in my Infancy in its primitive and innocent clarity was totally eclipsed: insomuch that I was fain to learn all again. If you ask me how it was eclipsed? Truly by the customs and manners of men, which like contrary winds blew it out: by an innumerable company of other objects, rude, vulgar, and worthless things, that like so many loads of earth and dung did overwhelm and bury it: by the impetuous torrent of wrong desires in all others whom I saw or knew that carried me away and alienated me from it: by a whole sea of other matters and concernments that covered and drowned it: finally by a bad education that did not foster and cherish it. . . . Had any man spoken of it, it had been the most easy thing in the world, to have taught me, and to have made me believe that Heaven and Earth was God's House, and that He gave it me.'

The study of Beauty in Nature has never been included in the school curriculum laid down by the Board of Education, but would it were possible for everyone interested and engaged in the work of children's education to ensure that a truer proportion of value should be set on the natural, the beautiful, the simple things of life. It is not enough to study the miracles of Nature by pulling the petals of a primrose apart in order to discover its botanical make-up, or to dissect a frog in order to learn its anatomical processes; but by contemplating the kaleidoscopic changes of the sky when the sun is bidding good night in a glory of vivid golds and reds: by rising early for the sole purpose of experiencing the fresh nip of a September morning and of watching the sun gradually gather together the smoky skirts of mist that lie on field and woodland, leaving every grass-blade and leaf endowered with a glistening diamond of dew in its heart—thus do we learn of the infinite wonder of the universe.

Surely there are few children of Dorset who would forsake their native county for the rigours and artificialities of town-life, or who could not be taught to appreciate the beauty that surrounds them? Such a wealth of charm, such a variety of type is to be found within its borders. Certainly it is one of the most unspoilt of English counties, and retains an atmosphere and a character quite unlike its neighbours. It has taken a share in the romance of its country's history: it has bred heroes: it is now playing no inconspicuous part in developing the experimental side of the New Agriculture, and yet it remains individual and detached. Sleepy it appears at first sight, but it is not too sleepy to be aware of the march of events in the world. Traffic whirls by, but it remains unmoved, rather like a wise old sheepdog in the sunshine of the wayside, who may raise his head for a moment to watch the pageant pass along, but will never lift a paw to join in a life other than that for which he was intended, to which he is dedicated. And Dorset men could not do better than consider themselves dedicated to life on the land in Dorset; the future is in their hands. The workers of to-day have stepped into a heritage battled and won for them by the valiant souls of yesterday, and the love of the land and their country still lives in their hearts as it lived in the hearts of their forebears, the Martyrs of Tolpuddle, one hundred years ago.